Return on Ideas

Return on Ideas

A practical guide to making innovation pay

David Nichols

BICENTENNIAL
1807
WILEY
2007
BICENTENNIAL

John Wiley & Sons, Ltd

Other Wiley Editorial Offices

John Wiley & Sons Inc., 111 River Street, Hoboken, NJ 07030, USA

Jossey-Bass, 989 Market Street, San Francisco, CA 94103-1741, USA

Wiley-VCH Verlag GmbH, Boschstr. 12, D-69469 Weinheim, Germany

John Wiley & Sons Australia Ltd, 42 McDougall Street, Milton, Queensland 4064, Australia

John Wiley & Sons (Asia) Pte Ltd, 2 Clementi Loop #02-01, Jin Xing Distripark, Singapore 129809

John Wiley & Sons Canada Ltd, 6045 Freemont Blvd, Mississauga, Ontario, L5R 4J3, Canada

Wiley also publishes its books in a variety of electronic formats. Some content that appears
in print may not be available in electronic books.

Library of Congress Cataloging-in-Publication Data

Nichols, David, 1967-
    Return on ideas : A practical guide to making innovation pay / David Nichols.
        p. cm.
    Includes bibliographical references and index.
    ISBN 978-0-470-02857-5 (cloth)
    1.   Product management. 2.   Brand name products. 3.   Diffusion of innovations.   I. Title.
    HF5415.15.N53 2007
    658.4 ′ 063 – dc22

                                                                                2007004233

British Library Cataloguing in Publication Data

A catalogue record for this book is available from the British Library

ISBN: 978-0-470-02857-5 (HB)

Typeset in 12/15pt Garamond by Laserwords Private Limited, Chennai, India
Printed and bound in Great Britain by Antony Rowe Ltd, Chippenham, Wiltshire
This book is printed on acid-free paper responsibly manufactured from sustainable forestry
in which at least two trees are planted for each one used for paper production.

for Clare, Holly and Imogen

Contents

About the Author   xiii

Acknowledgements   xv

1. **This is getting us nowhere**   1
   What is the problem? The Funnel   1

2. **How to navigate this book**   5
   Segmenting users   7

PART I: The Case Study   11

3. **The Calippo Shots story**   13
   Headlines   13
   The Ice Cream scene   14
   Starting with a clear vision   15
   Generate lots of high quality ideas   16
   Quickly getting down to the best ideas   18
   Building the best ideas into winning mixes   19
   After launch   20
   Key takeouts   20
   Handover   21

PART II: The Challenge   23

4. **Innovation isn't working**   25
   Headlines   25
   Innovation's the thing   25

Innovation isn't   28
Funnels Don't Work   29
Ten ways funnels stifle innovation   32
A dizzying conclusion   46
Key takeouts   53
Checklist: Is innovation being stifled by your funnel?   53
Handover   54

PART III: The Core Idea   **55**

5. A new innovation paradigm: The Rocket Motor   **57**
Headlines   57
Innovation is, in fact, Rocket science   58
Key takeouts   66
Handover   67

6. Rocketing: Destination   **69**
Headlines   69
Being clear   69
Hamster-wheeling   73
Begin with the end in mind   74
Key takeouts   91
Checklist : Destination   91
Handover   92

7. Rocketing: Combustion   **93**
Headlines   93
Not enough good ideas   93
7.1 Continuous Insight Fuel   95
    From insight to fuel   95
    360° Insight   96
    360° Insight Sources   97
7.2 Multiple Ignition In Parallel   110
    Igniting the insight fuel   110
    Parallel processing   110

Lisa and Mac   114
Practical Ignition Tools   115
7.3 3 Bucket Principle   128
What it is   128
Grave-robbing   131
7.4 Coda: A whole year view of Innovation   134
The 15% rule   134
Your typical year   134
Key takeouts   136
Checklist: Combustion   137
Handover   137

8. **Rocketing: Nozzle**   **139**
Headlines   139
From Whittle to 'Wow'   139
Picking winners is a lottery   140
Show business: Theatre Rules   143
Poor external screening   150
Show business: Idea Power   150
Key takeouts   157
Checklist: Nozzle   157
Handover   158

9. **Rocketing: Expander**   **159**
Headlines   159
Keeping positive   159
Innovation Antibodies   160
Expand not evaluate   161
Be a builder not a knocker   162
Execution is everything   170
Get real feedback   170
Launch then tweak   176
Key Takeouts   177
Checklist: Combustion   177
Handover   178

PART IV: The Entertainment   **179**

10. Ten innovations that make it look easy   **181**
Innovation shortcuts   181
New brands are innovations too   182
The 10 Innovations   183

PART V: The Practicalities   **205**

11. Doing it faster   **207**
Headlines   207
It always takes longer than you want it to   208
Case Study: Project Blues for Unilever Foods   209
The Approach   209
Plan in decisions   210
Smaller teams   212
Parallel Ideation   214
Real-time insight   216
Fast agencies   217
Blues: The result   218
Key takeouts   218
Checklist: Doing it faster   218
Handover   219

12. Avoiding the pitfalls   **221**
Headlines   221
Pitfalls and Pratfalls   222
Nine innovation pitfalls   223
No. 1: Oops, the product is useless   223
No. 2: 'Not invented here' syndrome   226
No. 3: The 'could it be. . . ?' killer   229
No. 4: Over-testing   231
No. 5: Killing by proxy   233
No. 6: The off-guard boss   235
No. 7: 'Yes, but. . .'   237
No. 8: Poor casting   238

No. 9: Giving up 240
Handover 242

Appendix: Rocketing toolkit 243

Index 255

About the Author

David Nichols is a marketing coach who "*makes us feel like we can achieve everything we want*" according to one of his global brand director clients. He teamed up with David Taylor in 2006 to become a Managing Partner of the brandgym, a consultancy that coaches teams to create a clear brand vision *and* the action plan to turn this into growth. He has led brand vision and innovation projects for many global companies and brands including Castrol, Vodafone, Unilever and Cadburys.

David is co-author of "*Brands & Gaming: The computer gaming phenomenon and its impact on brands and business*" published by Palgrave Macmillan in 2005, cataloguing the rise and rise of a new global cultural phenomenon that is going to change the marketing landscape forever.

He started his career at OC&C Strategy consultants, moving on to the marketing consultancy Added Value where he spent 11 years rising to be Managing Director of the UK, including stints in Paris and as MD in Australia.

David has written and produced three full scale musicals and managed a professional improv troupe, *The Impro Musical*, working with Tony Slattery, Eddie Izzard and Greg Proops.

He has a first class degree in Aerospace Engineering from Bristol University and in his spare time is an aerobatic pilot.

Contact David at davidn@thebrandgym.com

Acknowledgements

Without the marketing Directors, brand directors and brand managers with whom I was lucky enough to work over the last 12 years there would be no *Return on Ideas*. The projects that we did together stretching brands and building innovations are the bedrock of this book. The people in particular that I would like to thank for their time and contribution are Alan Martin at FayRouz (formerly Unilever Ice Cream), David Arkwright formerly at Unilever HPC, Mark Johnson at Mars Petfoods and Peter Boucher at Vodafone. Those who had a direct influence on some of the practical techniques in this book are Suthipa Panyamahasup and Carlo Mereghetti at Unilever Foods, Monique Carter at Pepsi, Richard Pash at Vodafone, Sally Bye and Linda Cripps at Castrol and Jason Warner at Beverage Partners Worldwide. Many other managers gave up valuable time to be interviewed and discuss case studies: Alan Hely at Apple, Caroline Neumann at Boehringer-Ingelheim, Andy Moore at Vodafone, Matt Adams at Pernod-Ricard, and Nick Green at Core Design. I must also mention the input from three first class qualitative research practitioners; Clare Greenwood, Louize Gibson and Kirstie Storrar, who's inspiring and insightful thinking has cracked many seemingly impossible innovation challenges with me.

The vast bulk of my work on innovation I did whilst working for Mark Sherrington and Peter Dart at Added Value, and it is to them that I extend my heartfelt thanks for their high standards, vast experience and constant challenge.

Innovation is nothing without creativity, and when in my darkest hours I needed a boost I turned to my creative partner Matt Avery, with whom I have written and produced 2 musicals, a computer gaming book and many terrible jokes, and he deftly provided the necessary creative juice for me to carry on.

The excellent illustrations were drawn by Simon Attfield at the talented packaging and innovation design agency SwaG Design (www.swagdesign.com) run by my friends Jon Miller and Dan Gallimore. Sarah Holland of Life Support took on the monster task of sorting out the many permissions and copyright approvals required for all the other images which she did with her usual amazing calm efficiency.

Above all I must thank my friend and partner at the brandgym, David Taylor. It was his idea in the first place that I should commit all my thinking on innovation into a book. He helped me structure it, gave me constant encouragement and honest feedback, to the point of telling me that if I was really finding it too hard I should just stop, which of course spurred me on to finish it. It was he who put me in touch with Claire Plimmer at Wiley & Sons, whose enthusiasm for the book and efficient team made the production process a joy. I am very proud to be contributing the fourth instalment in the brandgym series after David's three excellent books; *The Brandgym*, *Brand Stretch* and *Brand Vision*.

Lastly I must thank my wonderful wife Clare for her support, encouragement and forbearance during the writing process. As a marketing consultant with a fierce intelligence herself, her feedback over dinner and on my first draft were major factors in shaping the book. And she makes a mean Tarte Tatin, too!

This is getting us nowhere

CHAPTER 1

"All the armies in the world cannot resist an idea whose time has come."

Victor Hugo

I'll say it again.

This is getting us nowhere.

Time and time again marketers push off into yet another innovation project and come to grief on the same rocks. From financial services to fine wines, soft drinks to soap detergents and there is an alarming consistency in all of them; innovation isn't working. That's not to say no innovations happen or get launched, of course they do. But it's just so damned hard. More and more corporate resources are being funnelled into the quest for tomorrow's big innovation and it just isn't happening. It is costing more and more to develop each innovation and they are being no more successful.

Our chairmen are always talking up innovation as a core competence and how it will solve so many of the issues facing both the top and bottom line. It will transform low-margin, low-growth 'dog' categories and products into cash-generating superstars. With mounting competition from small nimble new entrants, the big players are finding themselves in a tighter and tighter corner. 'Innovate or die' is the mantra, but actually it should read: 'Innovate (faster and with fewer resources) or die.'

Investment in R&D is being focused on key areas, innovation teams are well staffed and research budgets are bigger than ever. But the innovation task still seems to be getting harder. Resources are being chewed up by the bucket load including, most importantly, internal energy and inspiration. But the final results are less than sparkling most of the time.

What is the problem? The Funnel

The key innovation process in major businesses today is the Innovation Funnel; the process of developing ideas in stages at the end of which is an evaluation that whittles the ideas down to a smaller number so that resources can be focused on fewer 'winners' in the next stage. It isn't working. In fact it seems to be inspiring low-quality ideas, making the whole process longer and more resource intensive and, ultimately, producing poor-quality output. If corporations want to grow both top and bottom lines consistently, then they need to fix it. Fast.

The alternative to the formal, admin-intensive Innovation Funnel that is held up as the way to break out of the innovation doldrums is to be a rebel; break all the rules and spearhead a drive to put yourself out of business before your competitors do by innovating entirely new markets. This is good, but not enough, and it can divert attention away from the core challenge which is to create growth in core markets with current brands. This is the real challenge for innovators, and it is more difficult to do than radical innovation because innovating the core has all the constraints of an existing business model heaped upon it.

There must a better way than either of these two approaches to deliver innovation in these hyper-competitive, over-saturated markets with marketing savvy cynical consumers.

There is. It's called Rocketing. It is formally introduced in Chapter 5 and explained in detail, step by step, in Chapters 6 to 9. Instead of focusing all efforts and resources on whittling down many ideas to a 'winner', Rocketing takes the analogy of a rocket motor and focuses on building ideas up to maximum impact at launch. Rocket motors are very simple, but very powerful, and make a good model for an innovation process that has to work within a major corporation. Rocketing is not intended as a total replacement for the Funnel, but as a reallocation of resources and an upgrading of the principles and methods used within it. There are fours stages to Rocketing:

- *Destination* – Being crystal clear on your goal is the first and crucial step in successful innovation.
- *Combustion* – Generating a larger number of high-quality ideas through continuous insight, multiple ideas generation and efficient ideas management.
- *Nozzle* – A swift prioritization of ideas, relying on experience and instinct together with powerful evaluation criteria, releases time and resource into the rest of the process.
- *Expander* – Building ideas into prototypes and 360° mixes earlier by focusing effort and energy on building ideas, not spotting problems.

With the tools and process laid out in these chapters you can turn your next innovation project into a quicker, more efficient process that will give you a greater chance of success as the end result.

The final chapters discuss the practicalities of Rocketing in the real world, such as the approaches to take if you really want to innovate quickly – not just cutting a chunk off the standard 18-month timeline, but doing the whole thing from start to finish in a few months. It's also necessary to avoid the pitfalls that inevitably crop up in every large organization – from getting past the "yes, but. . ." people in every meeting to avoiding ideas being stymied at birth 'by proxy' because someone doesn't think the boss will like them.

Innovation is the life-blood of branded business and today it is not delivering enough oxygen to the corporate heart. It's being stifled by too much admin, too many processes and too many corporate antibodies and it's got to stop. Your ideas deserve better.

There is a way of doing innovation that fits today's corporate cultures *and* produces successful ideas. This book is dedicated to laying out how you can get more for all the resource you put into innovation. In short, it tells you how to get a better return on your ideas.

How to navigate this book

CHAPTER 2

Start at the beginning and read to the end.

Well, that is one way to do it. It's perfectly valid, but a bit conventional. However, this book hasn't been written in a conventional, linear fashion, so you don't have to read it that way. It's only the constraints of analogue publishing that make it so singularly sequential. This book is written from the middle outwards (Figure 2.1), much in the way a workshop would be run on it; no long preamble or much of an introduction, just dive into the meat, get the principle of the idea explained, then go back and lay out the niceties of why the subject is important, what came before it, why it should be changed, etc. Chapters in a book

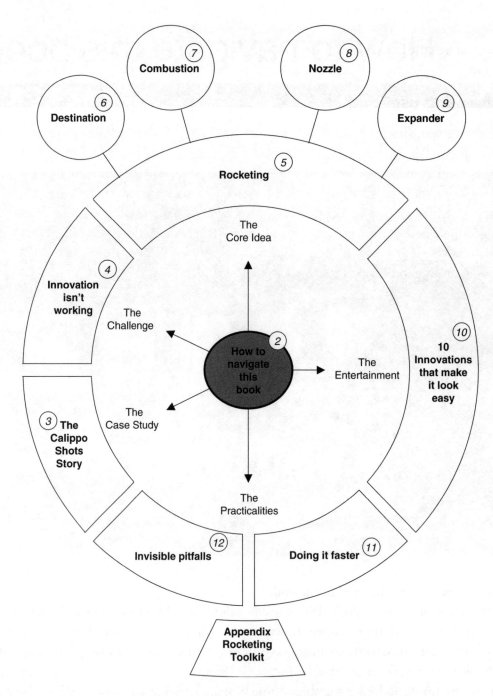

Figure 2.1: A map of this book.

don't seem to work very well like that. Instead, here is a short guide chapter on how you can get more out of the book by, perhaps, taking non-conventional routes into it.

Segmenting users

What people want from reading a business book very much depends on who they are and their situation. This is a phenomenon that most marketers should be very familiar with – it's called segmentation. Who you are, what mood you are in and how much time you have, all inform why you have picked up a business book and thus what you want from the experience of reading it. Like all good needs-based segmentations, this not about describing types you can pigeonhole people into, but an array of needs on specific occasions in which people can find themselves. If it's a good enough technique for targeting chocolate bars and mobile phones, then it's good enough for this book.

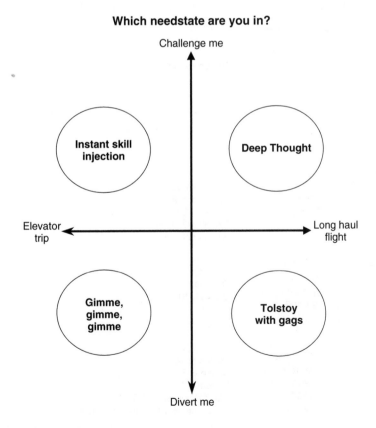

Figure 2.2: Reader Segmentation.

There are many ways in which you could segment potential readers, i.e. you. The five axes of segmentation, as outlined in my colleague David Taylor's first book *The Brand Gym*, are an excellent method, but too much of a long haul for what we need here. Instead, like a good film star, it's best to be short. The two axes that seem most meaningful are the time you have available and the principle need you have in picking up this book. The extremes of ordinary reading situations inform these axes. They are:

X-axis: Time available to read a business book

Shortest: Going up a couple of floors in the elevator to see the boss/agency/view.
Longest: On a flight to Australia, you can't sleep and the in-flight movies are not working.

Y-axis: Need when reading a business book

One extreme: To be diverted, but still appear to be working.
The other: A genuine desire to learn and develop yourself, perhaps immediately after your mid-year review.

Needstate	Recommended Chapters
Instant skill injection	Precis 7 Photocopy the Appendix
Deep thought	Paddle through 4 Dive into 5-9 Surf on 12 & the Appendix Dry off with 10 & 11 Jump back into 3
Gimme, gimme, gimme	Do some 5 Cut with 10
Tolstoy with gags	Munch on 4 Nibble at 3 Devour 5-9 Wash down with 10 & 11 Round off with 12 & the Appendix

Figure 2.3: How to navigate this book.

Plot these two against each other in the time-honoured fashion and behold, you have a simple segmentation that would make a trainee BCG consultant smile. Figure 2.2 lays out this segmentation and on it are plotted four reasonably plausible needstates that you might be finding yourself in now, as you read this book. For each, in Figure 2.3, there are suggestions on the route you might like to follow through this book.

But of course, as with all segmentations, a real person like you will simply ignore the carefully thought through strategic framework and read the book exactly as you please.

Be my guest.

The case study

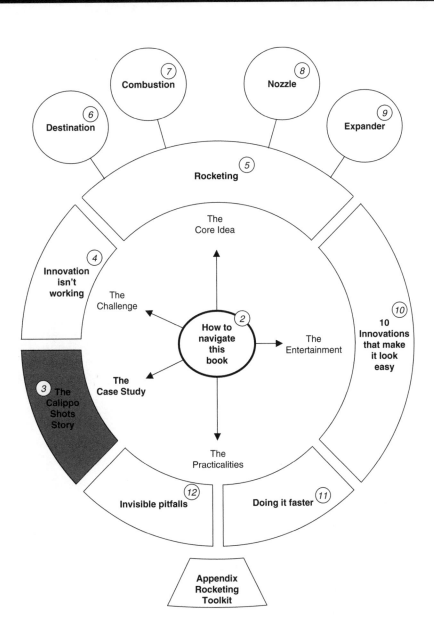

PART I

Combustion ⑦

Nozzle ⑧

Destination ⑥

Expander ⑨

Rocketing ⑤

The Core Idea

Innovation isn't working ④

The Challenge

How to navigate this book ②

The Entertainment

10 Innovations that make it look easy ⑩

③ The Calippo Shots Story

The Case Study

The Practicalities

Invisible pitfalls ⑫

Doing it faster ⑪

Appendix Rocketing Toolkit

The Calippo Shots story

CHAPTER 3

Figure 3.1: Calippo – the core product.

 Headlines

This is the story of a great innovation, one that took on an impossible task and delivered in spades. The process the team took was unorthodox for a large well-structured company. It was not a sequential step-by-step route through the standard innovation funnel. The team used new insight techniques, gave room for plenty of mistakes to be made, recycled ideas, used prototypes early and often, used experience and instinct to make their evaluations and worked intimately with R&D right from the start. In short, they innovated the innovation process and came up trumps with a product that changed the market it was launched into.

The Ice Cream scene

The ice cream market is large and Unilever Ice Cream is the largest player in it. Its umbrella brand is called different things across the world; Langnese in Germany, Frigo in Spain, Wall's in the UK, Kibon in Brazil to name a few, but has the same positioning everywhere. This offers some advantages in that it can dominate the freezer space and build global scale for its key brands. In the late 1990s their water ice brands did not attain the same popularity as their premium ice cream Magnum or family favourite Cornetto, but were nonetheless solid performers in a low-growth segment. The one strong brand they did have in water ice was Calippo and it was on this brand that Added Value was briefed to help create a breakout innovation. Calippo was a successful one product brand available in many countries which sold well to mums as a treat for their kids during the summer months. Analysis of the consumption data indicated that the kids were actually very young, 2 or 3 years old in some European markets. There seemed to be a slow decline in consumption up to the age of about 11 or 12 when it reached a complete cut off point.

Growth was required from all brands in the Unilever Ice Cream portfolio, to justify their place in the freezer cabinet, so the brand team had developed a new vision with the clear goal of unleashing growth and uncapping this 'glass ceiling' on the brand's consumption target. The vision was summarised as 'Freestyle Refreshment' – the refreshment of pure ice in a unique pack that's fun to play with in any way you want.

> **Freestyle Refreshment**
>
> The delicious water ice that gives you
> the refreshment of pure ice that's
> easy to eat your way

Figure 3.2: Calippo Brand Vision (author's own).

This vision gave the brand new momentum and focused growth on bringing in teenagers. To this end a great new advertising campaign had been developed with the tagline 'Do it your way' which captured the positioning very well. This was helping alter perceptions amongst teens, but the team knew this was only part of the answer. The fundamental stumbling block was that the product just didn't appeal to teens whose water ice consumption stopped as soon as they had their own money and begun buying soft drinks. The cool credentials and instant hit of refreshment offered by CSDs outdid the core Calippo tube on every level. Plus, Calippo was strongly associated with little kids – a 'no go' for self conscious teens. They realised they had to innovate something that leveraged the brand idea and took Calippo into head-on competition with soft drinks on their home turf – teen refreshment.

Starting with a clear vision

They started with this brand positioning and wrote themselves a detailed innovation brief, according to the required process. But they took it one step further and boiled their ambition down to a crystal clear, unequivocal challenge:

> ## Calippo – the innovation challenge
> - Target teens
> - Substitute soft drinks, not ice cream

They also promised that they would deliver the innovation in time for the following summer. In the ice cream business there are no late entries: either you are there for summer, which means bought and in stock at retailers and wholesalers by the end of March, or you are nowhere. This gave them a stark deadline that they had to meet or miss out on a year's worth of sales. Together, the deadline and the innovation challenge gave the team the strongest possible starting point: a clear vision of the end game. No vagaries here, no bland requests to simply increase share or hit broad volume targets. This was a tangible target that the team could see in glorious technicolour; a teen goes into a newsagent looking for refreshment with taste. On going to the fridge he or she sees Calippo XXX at the freezer, and buys that instead of the usual big brand can. This was a target that could be easily qualified by seeing if teens actually did buy it, and easily quantified by looking at substitution effects in teenagers' refreshment portfolios. At the other side of this challenge was ice cream; anything new in the freezer had to replace something already there – no extra shelf space is available when you are locked in a freezer that you supply yourself. This meant that to win through it had to have either a better margin per unit or a significantly higher rate of sale.

They decided on a small core team; the Marketing Manager to run the process reporting to the Marketing Director on a weekly basis, an R&D ice specialist, a lead market representative from Spain and a marketing agency as insight, process and consulting partner. For key meetings this involved a team of six, but for day-to-day issues, only two or three needed to get together.

The innovation process was designed by the team at the first meeting. This was an important point as, rather than getting an agency to pitch a research process and then running the innovation around it, the brand team chose the agency who had helped them to develop the brand vision, and they all set about designing the process together. This way it was innovative in two aspects: it involved some new things that no one had done before and it was left intentionally loose to accommodate new directions and ideas that emerged during the project.

Key success factors

- Strong brand positioning as guide
- Clear unequivocal innovation challenge, brought to life tangibly for the whole team
- Flexible process
- Small team
- Immovable deadline

Generate lots of high quality ideas

As they knew they had a tough task on their hands to take on the soft drinks giants, they needed lots of high-quality ideas. They tackled this in two ways.

Fresh insight

The team already knew a lot about ice refreshment need states from their research for the brand vision. They also collated internal knowledge of the soft drinks market from other parts of the business, such as the team working on Lipton Ice tea. What they found confirmed that soft drinks were indeed closer to water ice in refreshment terms than ice cream, which fell into more of a snacking, foody area for teens. They immediately briefed their R&D team to do a treasure hunt across all brands and past projects to see what product ideas they could suggest. What they now needed was some deeper insights into teenagers and their refreshment needs. The team decided to do something new and went headlong into an observation of teens and soft drinks. This was not a standard method of insight for Unilever but it yielded the critical insight. The team personally watched teenagers hanging around on their bikes with their friends drinking soft drinks from cans, or sucking or licking ice lollies. The results were enlightening: licking is a childish way to eat, swigging is for adults. Ice lollies put pressure on you to finish them before they melt, cans do not. Ice lollies are sticky and messy, cans are smooth and clean. All this amounted to the reason why, for teens, water ice was kiddy and cans were cool. See Figure 3.3.

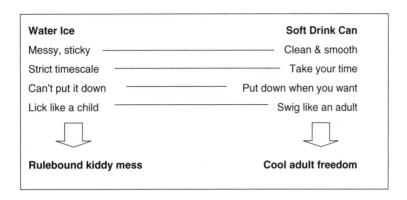

Figure 3.3: Insights from observation.

What it gave them was an even tighter brief. 'Good news' you might think, but it was an impossible brief.

Calippo impossible innovation brief	A water ice you can drink in a pack you can put down and reclose

Multiple ideation sessions

The team didn't flinch at this point and instead turned to their R&D department. What they didn't now about ice wasn't worth knowing. An ideation session was set up where they brought along every ice concoction conceivable, and plenty that were inconceivable too; soft ice, hard ice, bi-phase ice – you name it, they could do it, apart from ice you could drink. This was preceded by a looser ideas session done by the agency with external creatives and designers that produced 20–30 roughly sketched ideas, some of which were just bonkers (e.g. a doughnut-shaped pack with ice in friction-free continuous motion around it). At this point the team went further off-*piste* and decided to get teens creating ideas too. They set up brainstorming sessions in the UK and Spain with 16–18 olds, using some of the ideas from the internal sessions as thought starters, but leaving the scope wide open. The result of all these sessions was a huge number of interesting ideas. Among all these the team focused on 15–20 that felt really promising as they addressed the challenge from a number of different directions; some were packaging led, others had strong insights and some were based around a specific product. Just to be sure, all the ideas that had been around at the start of the project were reviewed for any further value they could bring to the top 20. The product team in the mean time had gone away to create the impossible 'drinkable ice' and came back with sludgy ice – so sweet that it dissolved teeth almost on contact. It was not very promising.

A load of balls

It was at this point that serendipity struck in the form of the team from Frigo, Unilever's Spanish Ice Cream business. A developer there had been experimenting in the factory and arrived at the ideas review and build session clutching a big bag of very small ice balls. The team tried various things, adding them to vodka, throwing them at each other, but when they were poured into a paper cup – the type you get at water coolers – the lights went on. Here was ice that you could drink. Even though it was solid ice, when in the form of lots of little balls, it behaved just like a liquid, and the concept of a cup full of little ice balls was formed.

Key success factors

- Fresh insights from a totally new perspectives
- Wide range of insight sources
- Multiple ideation sessions run simultaneously
- Visualizing ideas at the start
- Recycling of ideas

Quickly getting down to the best ideas

The agency went into overdrive bringing each of the top 10 ideas to life with product and pack sketches. A round of concept development research across Europe showing consumers pack sketches, written concepts and prototype products confirmed that three ideas, including the 'cup full of little balls', had real potential. When it came to present the ideas at the concept review after the qualitative stage, the marketing manager worked hard with the agency to bring the ideas to life in even more detail. They didn't just present PowerPoint concepts, but also digital illustrations of how the pack could appear. They also projected forward a few years and showed what possible extensions there could be, as well as new and interesting flavour combinations. In short, they had a bit of fun. In the review they also took a look at the business side of each idea and concluded that there were no significant negatives for the three leading ideas, only unanswered questions. The result was that out of the 10 ideas that had gone into the qualitative phase, they now had three that were much stronger than any others. Did they do a quantitative concept test to confirm what they already knew? No. They trusted their instincts and experience, preferring to move ahead at pace rather than effectively stop the project to wait for a slow expensive piece of quantitative work to tell them nothing new. All three leading ideas were turned into their own development projects. The one they tackled first now had the name of Calippo Shots.

> ## Key success factors
>
> - Mix of experience, gut instinct and consumer feedback used to identify strongest ideas
> - Ideas brought to life and presented with visuals and mix ideas, even at this early stage
> - Prioritization done swiftly

Building the best ideas into winning mixes

Now that the focus was exclusively on Calippo Shots (Figure 3.4), the design agency went to work on numerous ways to structure a pack that could be reclosed, put down and stacked in the manufacturing process. Again, a near impossible but clear brief yielded great results. The simple answer was an upside down cup – stackable in manufacturing terms, stable when put down, and all it needed was an expensive bespoke reclosable lid to deliver on the 'like a soft drink' brief. This could easily have been a project stopper. The internal view was that this kind of thing had never been done before in the freezer, was too expensive and too difficult to achieve. The team stood their ground and persevered with the designers and packaging suppliers, creating prototype after prototype to find the solution. Eventually their

Figure 3.4: Calippo Shots.

determination paid off and they found a way to make the lid work, despite the 'nay-sayers' and 'yes, but-ters' they encountered along the way.

Time for launch was getting close and they needed concrete prediction of its performance in the marketplace. Again, they went for the unorthodox route. Instead of an expensive and complex Simulated Test Market, they leveraged their personal contacts and launched the product in a real test market in an area of Australia. The results were better than they could have hoped for – it outsold everything in the ice cream cabinet by a factor of 3. Furthermore, the source of gains for this new innovation was not the various ice creams, and was not even current Calippo consumption. It was stealing directly from soft drinks.

Key success factors

- Mindset of problem solving, not flaw spotting
- Prototyping again and again until it was right
- Never giving up
- Real test market, not a simulated test market

After launch

It was launched in key European markets first, where the brand was most established and particularly in the market where it already had some teen consumers – Spain. A problem occurred with the bottom of the pack becoming unstuck and depositing the product directly into the laps of the consumer. This was jumped upon and a solution was found by changing the material from waxed card to plastic, which brought with it the added benefit of being transparent. Suddenly one of the early ideas for a multi-fruit variety with different coloured balls became possible. This has now been launched as the first line extension.

Before Shots was rolled out globally, Calippo came under the large strategic review of brands that Unilever was undertaking and it was decided that there was only to be one global refreshment based brand – Solero. Calippo Shots was duly rebranded to Solero Shots in most markets in the late 1990s. The latest situation is that, in some markets, Solero Shots has now been rebranded back to Calippo Shots. Either way the innovation won the Unilever global innovation award and is now a multi-million dollar global success.

Key takeouts

1 Have a clear vision for your innovation.
2 Dramatize it tangibly for the whole team (even if it seems impossible).

3 Seek insight from fresh perspectives, going beyond your comfort zone.

4 Turn the insight into lots of high-quality ideas through multiple ideation sessions while working with R&D from the start and using visuals and prototypes.

5 Don't just present your ideas, give them as much life as possible and perform them at key review sessions.

6 Prioritize the best ideas swiftly, based on experience mixed with consumer feedback.

7 Focus on solving problems and building ideas up, not spotting flaws.

8 Stick with it – determination is as important as inspiration.

9 Once launched, keep tweaking to perfect the mix.

Handover

This case encapsulates the key themes and points from this book. Each of the key success factors is explained in detail and put within practical structures that you can apply to your own innovation projects. But firstly it's important to look at innovation more broadly and ask why it appears not to be working for most people most of the time and therefore why we need to rethink it.

The Challenge

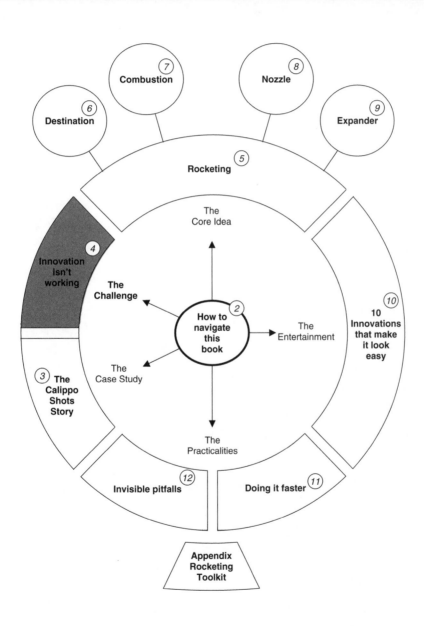

PART II

Innovation isn't working

CHAPTER 4

"People see the wrongness in an idea much quicker that the rightness."
Charles Kettering

 ## Headlines

Innovation is the magic dust that all businesses need to thrive in today's ultra-competitive markets. It has never been more central to the CEO's agenda. But success rates are dismal and not improving despite the scrutiny heaped upon the idea development process. The culprit is the Innovation Funnel. The very process put in to make innovation more of a certainty is making it more of a dead duck; stifling it with bureaucracy, poor decision making and a focus on picking faults not building competence. The alternative mooted by books is to be a rebel, tear up the rule book and reinvent your business from the ground up. This is fine for brilliant mavericks or bored billionaires, but won't do for core brands in core markets that need to carve out growth day in and day out. There has to be a better way.

Innovation's the thing

Innovation today is on every CEO's lips, every Chairman's speech notes and every marketing director's 'to do' list. It has become the business axiom of our generation, the torch-bearer of progress and the driving force of change. Not tectonic societal or political change, but the everyday bubbling of life and culture feeding a seemingly insatiable desire for the new and the different. In business, if you're not innovating, you're dead.

'The engine of real economic growth is not technology but innovation.'
Hector Ruiz, CEO, Advanced Micro Devices

If you are a CEO then you had better have a pretty good innovation story to tell your shareholders.

'The only source of profit, the only reason to invest in companies in the future is their ability to innovate and their ability to differentiate.'
Jeffrey Immelt, CEO of GE

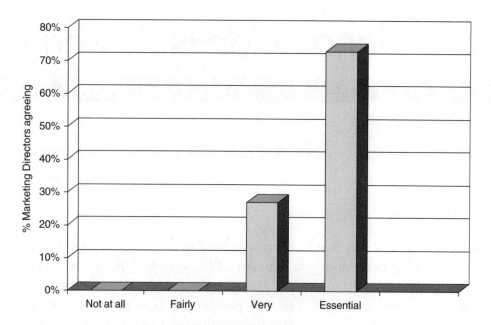

Figure 4.1: The Importance of Innovation for growth.

Source: Brandgym Research.

Innovation is increasingly held up as *the* solution to business issues, anything can in principle be conquered by the smart thinking and cunning reallocation of resources that innovation can achieve. It can turn low margin categories into profit stars – just look at Ryanair's results in the beleaguered post-9/11 airline industry. It can create growth in declining markets – margarine in the UK is a large category that has been in decline for more than 5 years, Unilever's Flora Pro-Activ innovation bucked the trend and has been in double-digit growth every year. Marketing directors are also crystal clear on innovation's role in delivering corporate growth, as shown in Figure 4.1.

Speed is good

Not only is innovation critical, it is needed urgently. Innovation is taking too long in big companies. Smaller competitors are getting there first too often. Standard idea-to-launch timelines of 2–3 years are no longer delivering first-mover advantage. Nimbler, unencumbered competitors are outmanoeuvring the multinationals on an almost daily basis. Who was first to introduce current account mortgages? The big banks? No. It was the new entrants, like Virgin in the UK, who innovated first. Who first delivered reliable, easy to use mobile email to business users? The big mobile players? No. It was a start-up company

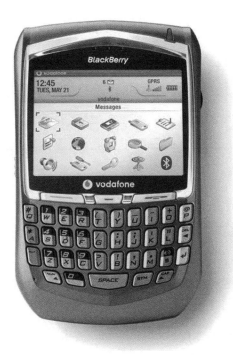

Figure 4.2: RIM Blackberry™ beat the big companies to mobile email.

The RIM and BlackBerry® families of related marks, images and symbols are the exclusive properties of and trademarks of Research In Motion – used by permission.

called Research In Motion that introduced the Blackberry (Figure 4.2), which is still the lead player in hardware and software. Even if major corporates' new ideas are really good, they still might fail unless they are delivered to market as fast as a new entrant.

Increasing scrutiny

As a result of this situation innovation has come under an unprecedented amount of scrutiny. The business process engineers have pored over the workings of Marketing, R&D, Research and countless other departments. They have been installing and perfecting ways to make innovation more effective. All manner of management information systems have sprung up to quantify innovativeness; from softer organizational cultural measures like 'openness to new ideas', to harder quotas like specific return on innovation investment targets. All these and more are popping up on CEO's radars. Greater accountability, greater efficiency and greater effectiveness are the goals they're after because they know that doing innovation better will drive sustainable sales growth and profits.

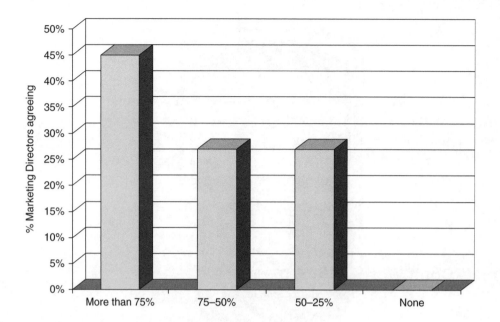

Figure 4.3: Proportion of Innovation projects that fail.

Source: Brandgym research.

But it's just not happening.

Innovation isn't

You don't need me to tell you that innovation success rates are low. For most companies, most of the time, innovation is not happening faster, more efficiently or more successfully. In fact, it's quite the opposite. It's getting worse. More resources, energy and time are being spent innovating than ever before, and the results are dismal. Only 50% of brand extensions survive after three years (Taylor, 2004).[1] If you expand this to include all new brand launches and business start-ups – the numbers get worse.

And this poor hit rate is just for those that get launched.

How about all the innovation projects that fail to deliver new products or services that are worthy of launch? Research by the Brandgym, shown in Figure 4.3, shows that approximately half of all innovation projects fail to deliver the ideas that are launched. And that is shining a pretty positive light on the numbers. The real proportion of failures could be nearer two-thirds.

---

[1]see Taylor, D. (2004) *Brand Stretch: Why 1 in 2 Extensions Fail and How to Beat the Odds.* Chichester: John Wiley & Sons.

It's a lottery

This means that as you set about your next innovation project, dreaming of the golden day when the CEO slaps you on the back and says 'well done' for turning around the company's fortunes with your brilliant idea, the actual chances of your delivering something that will last longer than three years are . . . well, incredibly small.

But surely the least we can do is make a success of the bit we totally control. Why should the process of developing ideas from within the safety of our own businesses be as hazardous an endeavour as launching them into the shark-infested waters of the twenty-first century marketplace?

Innovation Funnels are to blame.

Funnels Don't Work

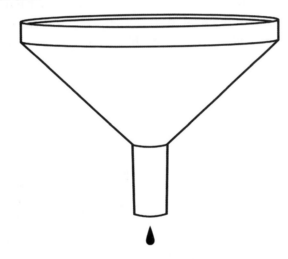

Why Funnels?

Innovation Funnels were introduced to improve the innovation process, and make it more efficient. The objectives were broadly:

1 To introduce a best practice method that could raise the quality of every project.
2 To split innovation into clear steps that could be measured and thus provide management with information on overall progress and efficiency.
3 To channel investment and precious company resources into fewer more successful ideas.

The funnel methodology is to be found in many major branded businesses across many different markets. I have seen it in action in soft drinks, OTC pharmaceuticals, salty snacks, confectionery, pet food, beer, wine, spirits, ice cream, personal care, detergents, yoghurts and many more. The process may vary in how it is executed between companies, but the basic configuration is consistent.

How funnels work

At the heart of the Innovation Funnel – its inner workings – is the 'stage-gate system' (see Figure 4.4). Developed by Robert Cooper in the late 1980s,[2] this methodology splits the funnel into several stages of development work with gates or checkpoints at the end of each where decisions are made on whether a project or idea should be killed off or allowed to proceed to the next stage.

The system works to allocate resources only to those ideas that have potential, whittling them down until only most commercial ideas are left to be launched. "The gradual process of reducing uncertainty through a series of problem solving stages" is the definition stated

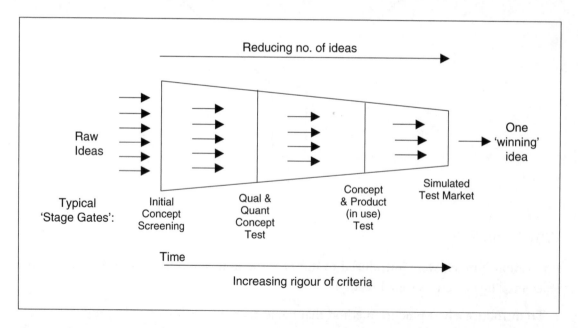

Figure 4.4: How funnels work.

---

[2]Harvard Business Essentials (2003) *Managing Creativity to Innovation*. Harvard Business School Press.

by Joe Tidd and colleagues in *"Managing Innovation"*.[3] The intention of the funnel is clear – to reduce the number of ideas from many at the start to a few 'winners' at the end. In the excellent book *Managing Creativity & Innovation*[2] this is stated as a process of 'killing' ideas:

> The quicker a company can kill off the ideas that won't make it to commercialization, the less the costs will be. Quick kills have the virtue of making more resources available for the handful of ideas that have real merit.

The basic idea is to progress only those ideas that tick all the boxes (e.g. feasible, big potential) so that resource is only used where it will most likely bear fruit. This amounts to a systematic, accountable whittling down of ideas to find a 'winner'. This is a very sensible system in principle, but in practice the approach is not producing better ideas or more successful innovations. Even the underlying semiotic meaning of a funnel is inconsistent with innovation; squeezing out, constricting, reducing, controlling – all the opposite of creation, inspiration and explosive growth that should typify an innovation success. Is it any wonder that funnels are putting a downer on idea development when the very body language of the process is so counterproductive?

The idea-killing machine is working too well. Funnels are stifling innovation.

---

[3]Tidd, J., Bessant, B. B Pauth, K. (2001) *Managing Innovation* (2nd edition). Chichester: John Wiley & Sons.

Ten ways funnels stifle innovation

Focus is on picking winners not creating winners

The entire focus of the funnel and stage-gate process is to 'whittle down' a large number of ideas to a smaller number by 'killing off' weaker ones and 'picking' the winners. All the effort and the thinking is on removing ideas, spotting weaklings and finding faults, rather than being constructive and finding solutions to the problems that each idea poses. A great example of constructive thinking, of using problems as stimulus for improving ideas, is Kellogg's Coco Pops. When the team tasked with developing a new kids' cereal offer for Kellogg's created the idea of chocolate-covered Rice Krispies, they kept hitting a product problem. R&D worked hard but they couldn't find an easy, cheap way of making the chocolate coating stay on the Rice Krispies. When it was put in milk – it all fell off. Instead of going back to the drawing board, the team took it as a challenge to find an ingenious solution – so they thought like kids. The answer was suddenly obvious: "New Coco Pops, so chocolately, it even turns the milk into chocolate milk!". The 'problem' became a key part of the launch of a huge success.

At a standard evaluation stage-gate the focus would have been on marking this concept down as it had a manufacturing 'problem'. This deconstructive mindset gets reinforced at every gate and can easily pervade the whole system.

Admin is at the core, not ideas

The funnel process brings with it a huge paper load, one that is getting bigger not smaller. As companies put more and more expectations on their innovation, so too do they measure it more. It must be efficient, accountable and best-in-class and thus it must be documented. Otherwise what will the management consultants pore over when they advise on business process re-engineering to increase innovation efficiency?

An accountability-free innovation process is not the goal. Far from it. But with no counteractive force, the weight and influence of data and admin can take over. This is very dangerous because when ideas are so new and ill formed the data we can get is at best 'iffy'. The designers of the funnel system said that companies have to be comfortable with a lack of data at these early development stages. In their book[4] W. Chan Kim and Rénee Mauborgne say very rightly that you can't size a market that does not yet exist, and, equally, a half-formed one-page concept should not be treated like a real contender to existing offers. When admin takes over and data is the only voice, ideas are killed off too easily. The other thing that happens, highlighted very well by Clayton M. Christensen is his book,[5] is that data-led innovation evaluation tends to favour the familiar. Concepts that are close to the existing product get scored higher than new, difficult, strongly different ideas. Flavour variants suddenly become very appealing – you can predict how they will perform quite accurately. That, however, is a non-sensical reason to favour them over newer ideas. Isn't it?

[4]W. Chan Kim & Renee Mauborgne (2005) *Blue Ocean Strategy: How to create uncontested market space and make competition irrelevant,* Harvard Business School Press.
[5]Clayton M. Christensen (1997) *The Innovators Dilemma: When new technologies cause great firms to fail,* Harvard Business School Press.

Promotes 'Not invented here' syndrome

Figure 4.5: Apple iPod. The product of open, collaborative innovation.

If there ever was a company destined to own a whole new category it was Sony and portable digital music players. They owned the world's leading brand in the portable music market, Walkman; they also had all the technological expertise in storage, file formatting, user interface, consumer electronics design and distribution. They had all the retailer relationships you could wish for, yet they muffed it, big time. Why? One of the key reasons has to be their insistence on only using bespoke components, developing their own software (not their strong suit) and building it around their own proprietary file format, ATRAC – not the common MP3 format. The result is that this – two full years after iPod's launch (see Figure 4.5) – is the first time they have managed to release a player that accepts MP3 files. Even so, they still have to be irritatingly converted before they can be played. This is a company being killed by the 'not invented here' syndrome.

Funnels promote this kind of behaviour. When several concepts are in the funnel, it is all too easy for teams to show how 'mine is different' in order to get picked as the winner over your internal competitor. When a concept leverages in-house technology or proprietary software, it gets scored very highly in internal evaluation and that often enables it to pass through to the next stage instead of some other idea that does not use proprietary ingredients. This is a zero sum game.

Apple make it look easy. With one clear goal for all – launch a drop-dead gorgeous MP3 player on a specific date – they put all their energy into **building** one central concept, **solving** problems that arise and **stealing/sharing/using** ideas from wherever they come from to add value to it.

Funnels promote 'mine is better than yours' competitive bickering and thus waste resource and distract focus from the end goal (see Figure 4.6).

Apple iPod	Sony HD Walkman
• iTunes software bought from third party (SoundJam) • Hard drive a standard Toshiba component • Rest of components taken off the shelf from suppliers • Design: Apple	• Sony proprietary SonicStage software • Bespoke Sony components • Only runs Sony proprietary ATRAC format, mp3 files need 'converting' • Design : Sony
Launch: Q1 2002 **Sales:** Global no.1	**Launch:** Q4 2004 **Sales:** Distant no.2 or 3 with Scandisk

Figure 4.6: The Apple iPod vs. the Sony HD Walkman.

Makes it take longer

How long does it take to have an idea? Not long. It takes a little longer to get the right conditions and the right inspirational inputs set up. What takes the real time is evaluation and justification. Writing up **why** the idea is worthy of resources for development and **proving** that it has potential can take twice to 10 times longer than concocting the idea in the first place. It's time you took a quick test. In Figure 4.7 there is an innovation timesheet. Take a minute to fill it in and see how you fare.

What is your ratio? 2 to 1, 5 to 1? The ratio is probably nearer 10 to 1, admin to creativity. It's the nature of the stage-gate system itself that creates this imbalance and thus what is, in principle, a simple (but challenging) process becomes a much longer and more arduous one. Stage-gate systems currently overweight the admin side and make the whole process take longer than it should. In these days of own-label copycat-ing and internet business models, speed is an essential competitive tool you cannot afford to squander so readily.

In your last innovation project, how much time did you spend on the following:	**Days**
1. Generating and crafting ideas	☐
2. Evaluating and testing ideas	☐
3. Writing justifications	☐
4. Presenting ideas 'for info' to committees/other departments	☐
Total creativity (1)	☐
Total Admin (2 + 3 + 4)	☐
Ratio	——

Figure 4.7: The innovation timesheet.

Senior expertise focused on evaluation not improvement

In your last few innovation projects, were the most senior and experienced R&D, marketing or operations people involved or asked for their opinions? It may have been in an up front interview to get their views, but most likely it was at an important 'Go/No go' meeting and evaluation point. Their experience and expertise was being called upon to do one thing: spot the flaws. Which ideas won't work, won't go down the manufacturing line or won't pass muster with the retailer? Which concepts contain hidden costs or unforeseen problems further into their development? Spot the weaklings and weed them out, that's the job. This is no doubt a valuable task; being aware of future problems or potential hidden costs is good, it could help to avoid awkward delays later on. But is this the best value that these venerable people can bring to your project?

William L. McKnight was the charismatic and inspirational CEO of 3M who laid down a cultural pattern for innovation that is the foundation of their success. He created a culture that encouraged initiative and allowed anyone who proposed an original idea to try it and do more 'experimental doodling'. He strongly advocated giving people authority and responsibility for developing their own ideas – to let them do it their own way. He then clearly understood his role and the role of senior management in directing these individuals. As he wrote in 1948:

> Mistakes will be made. But if a person is essentially right, the mistakes he or she makes are not as serious in the long run as the mistakes management will make if it undertakes to tell those in authority exactly how they must do their jobs. Management that is destructively critical when mistakes are made kills initiative. And it's essential that we have many people with initiative if we are to continue to grow.

His notion of experimental doodling went on to become 3M's famous but unofficial '15 percent rule', which allows technical and scientific employees to use 15% of their time to pursue ideas of their own.

Would it not be better to focus the inputs of senior people into **solving** problems thrown up by new ideas such as: How can we get this to go down our line? What cost savings does this new idea allow versus our existing product?

Funnels don't demand this kind of input, but they do demand strict evaluation, flaw-spotting and the systematic weeding out of ideas with weak links. Would Bill McKnight approve?

Adds cost

How much does it cost to come up with an idea? Nothing or several millions? Even though there are undoubtedly many management accountants who have attempted to answer this question, the answer is meaningless. But one thing that's sure is that developing an idea through a stage-gate funnel process costs more than it needs to. Funnels are there to weed out the underperformers. They are designed to do it systematically, traceably and with defendable logic. That is why the decision between two fairly similar concepts – one of which suggests that a blue product colour cues increased efficiency and the other indicates that a green product colour does it better – requires a detailed, nationally representative comparable, repeatable and totally objective quantitative study with a control cell of the existing concept to provide an answer. These, unsurprisingly, are very expensive and time consuming. It is this need for certainty, in an area where there is no certainty, that relentlessly triggers more and more tests such as these, not all of which are needed and few of which actually add any value or shed real insight onto the issue. The result is that costs rise but idea impact stays the same.

Innovation by numbers

As the saying goes: 'Power corrupts, but absolute power corrupts absolutely.' The same could be said for innovation funnel processes. When the process takes over and simple sense gets left behind, then crazy things can happen.

In 2005 I was working with a team tasked with developing a major global innovation for a multi-billion dollar flagship brand in household cleaning. A concept had been crafted and the arduous process of developing the launch mix had begun. The team leader had sensibly recruited representatives from the key disciplines onto the team; product performance, visual cues, graphical design, structural packaging and fragrance. She had assembled them for a series of global review meetings together with the global marketing team and market research manager. As this represented a relaunch of the core product, a lot was riding on it and there were many constraints. The team were making headway none the less and were meeting in Brazil to look at the latest mock-ups of the potential mix. One of the most significant changes, from the consumer's point of view, was going to be adding a window to the pack, so the product could be seen at the point of purchase. This afforded an opportunity to differentiate against the competition and a chance to show off visual efficacy cues **before** purchase. This would of course raise packaging costs, but not very significantly in all regions. The packaging representative stated: "This will take 1 million dollars of capex to do, and to get sign off for that amount of money, we have to prove that the change would create a significant enough return." A sensible enough position for the manufacturing team to take, you might think. But wait: how exactly do you prove that a product window alone drives incremental sales higher? The answer is to do a side-by-side quantitative comparison test, of course. The meeting continued as the Market Research manager went about planning the new test into the time plan. There was already going to be a quantitative concept test, to get stage-gate approval, but that one didn't require finished packs. As it was a global innovation the multi-cell test was gong to cost $600,000 to cover all key markets and give confidence to everyone to invest in it. Now a second test was duly loaded in, across the same markets, but with packaging. This added an extra $600,000 and three months to the time plan.

The Market Research manager presented the second test and revised time plan after lunch and all agreed that this would secure their pack window which they felt was critical to the concept. This is when I spoke up: "You have just agreed to spending $1.2 million dollars (with immediate sign off) on market research to get approval for a $1 million dollar capex change so that this concept will get through to launch."

Their response?

"That's just the way it is." All the boxes would be ticked. All investments ratified and approved. Their idea would be no better for it but it would cost them three months and an armful of cash.

Just nuts.

It does cost money to come up with good ideas – sometimes a lot of money. Funnels, however, drive people to spend even more money convincing themselves that their ideas are good, whether they are or not. They make innovation more expensive than it should be.

Assumes good ideas are easy to come by

When an innovation funnel is drawn there are always loads of arrows coming in at the larger end representing ideas. Where do they come from? They just seem to appear by magic, as if it's the easiest thing in the world to concoct ideas to fill a funnel. As far as the funnel is concerned it doesn't matter where they come from, the process is utterly indiscriminate in its entry criteria for initial ideas. Well, that's good, isn't it? We shouldn't be screening ideas at birth, should we? And as to the source of ideas, that's just a matter of doing a brainstorming session. Don't they always produce tons of output?

Er . . . no.

The issue here is one of **quality**. Anyone can come up with 100 ideas for innovating, say, a yoghurt – let's make it blue, taste of eels, smell like deodorant, etc. – but how easy is it to come up with the idea of putting the fruity bit in the corner, separately, so that people can mix it in for themselves? How about coming up with 25 ideas of that quality? Not so easy.

Funnels are open to any ideas, and tend to get filled with any old ideas. They all get dutifully worked up into neatly typed concepts and suddenly everything looks ship shape ... to an accountant. Any marketer worth his salt should be able to sort the wheat from the chaff, but funnels are not run on instinct, they are run to a process, a system and to objective evaluation at stage-gates. That's why they seem to work as if they were run by accountants, not marketers.

A scene from a typical global marketing meeting reviewing innovation progress is shown in Box 4.1. Names have been changed to protect the guilty.

Generating ideas is somehow a low-status affair in innovation funnel process. You can avoid having any kind of process, if you want to. Senior managers seldom come to brainstormings – and why is that? Surely it is the most important part of the process? Because no matter how good your process for development, if your input is bad then your output

---

Box 4.1: A funnel full

MD:	Right, innovation review. I want to know how we're doing on developing 3 big innovations over the next two years. Simpkins, the funnel.
Simpkins:	Right. [Projection of impressive PowerPoint chart showing a funnel simply crammed with ideas.] We have confidence we can deliver; our funnel is full of ideas.
MD:	Full of ideas. Excellent
Simpkins:	Each individually captured in our proprietary Big Idea™ concept pro-forma.
MD:	Good work, Simpkins. I can see we're on our way to a timely delivery here.
Simpkins:	Yes we are.
MD:	Well, I'll leave you to it ... but before I go, show me one.
Simpkins:	Eh?
MD:	An idea, show me. Bit of fun to take into lunch with the CEO. What's that one? [MD points to one concept 'dot' on screen.]
Simpkins:	Er ... that's the family pack.
MD:	Oh, well what about that one?
Simpkins:	Yes, that's new, it's ... er ... the summer promotion pack. Oh.
MD:	That one?
Simpkins:	This year's launch, should have deleted it.
MD:	This one?
Simpkins:	Just been cancelled.
MD:	The rest?
Simpkins:	A product reformulation - legal reasons. Special size for Airlines. Five different packs for Luxembourg. The Christmas 'foot long' version. Logo changes for all 12 countries and a closure change to stop leaks in transit.
MD:	Ah.
Simpkins:	Oh, hang on, here's one. This one is a new concept.
MD:	At last! What is it?
Simpkins:	'Now available in Orange flavour.'

will also be bad. So, one of the most well-known and fundamental innovation principles states:

> ## CRAP IN = CRAP OUT

Wastes ideas

Funnels are a one-way street. If an idea is not chosen as a winner it gets spurned and rejected. In fact, the wastage rates are astronomical. In a typical project you might start with, say, 25 ideas coming from of a sparky productive brainstorming session. As you travel through the funnel process you are joining, say, three other similarly endowed projects – giving 100 ideas in the funnel. At the end, how many get launched? One, two, maybe three? At best, that's a 97% wastage rate! Any factory manager would be fired on the spot for running a line with that kind of efficiency.

In fact, in every other part of a business there are systems in place and a lot of effort is expended to extract maximum value from all resources: recycling, re-using and converting waste into secondary fuels. But not in innovation. The process that is held up as the source of growth, and the central engine of future profits, is a wastrel of the worst kind when it comes to one of the most precious resources we have: ideas.

> *Success has many fathers; failure is always an orphan.*

No one wants to be associated with failure. Concepts and ideas that don't make the grade or have had a flaw pointed out are abandoned like an unsafe building. No one ever wants to revisit them for fear of being tarred with the failure brush. This abhorrence of not being a winner leads to some precious resource being discarded that still has value to add. Funnels have no process or system for extracting the value from spent ideas, nor even for capturing them.

That makes me quite angry. So . . .

I am starting an active protest group to campaign against the wanton waste of marketing's most precious resource . . .

Brainchild

A positive action group set up to protect and nurture young ideas cruelly abandoned before they can add value

---

Our first action is to send a petition to the G7 leaders for a substantial grant to further our economic crusade. With these funds we will send a 'Bounty' style pack to the birthplace of new ideas: marketers. The pack will contain the following:

- Instant idea capturing device (Post-It™ pad and marker pen)
- Idea safe haven (A4 folder)
- A copy of this book.

It will be sent to every marketing graduate trainee as their induction pack into the global ideas economy.

If *you* would like to join, an application form is presented in Box 4.2

Box 4.2: Application to join Brainchild – the campaign against ideas wastage

Brainchild
The campaign against ideas wastage

Membership Application Form

Name: _____

Role: _____

Company: _____

I pledge my support to new ideas everywhere ☐

I offer a safe in-tray free from critical evaluation as a haven for ideas wantonly rejected and seeking succour ☐

I await my slogan T-shirt ☐ ☐ ☐
                           S   M   L

"Want to save ideas?
Stop me and ask how"

Please photocopy, fill in and send to:

Brainchild –Ideas Care Unit, 106 Dora Road, London SW19 7HJ

Demands no insight

Remember the story of the drunk and the lamppost? He only uses it for support, not for illumination. And so it is when we misuse insight. The funnel process demands multiple lampposts to be used to stay standing – but they could just as well all be switched off. No illumination is required here. The funnel process does not drive marketers to use their research budgets digging for more insights when a concept doesn't make it. Instead, it requests that the concept be killed off, or that money be spent to retest it. The emphasis of all research within the funnel is not for finding insight to improve ideas, but to find faults.

Creates gaps in marketing plans

We've seen how funnels make innovation take longer than necessary. We have also seen how easily funnels get filled with ideas indiscriminately, so that the average quality is at best uneven and, at worst, very low. These two aspects, when combined with the other failings of the process, add up to an **increased likelihood of failure**. This is not just ideas being a flop at launch, but innovation projects failing to produce ideas good enough to warrant a launch at all. This, of course, means that projects either stall completely or have to be restarted in a new direction or with new stimulus, but either way they slip significantly.

This means that marketing plans, built around key innovation launches, fall apart. Suddenly a well-balanced and aggressive brand growth plan, agreed with senior management in the business planning cycle, becomes a plan with a gap. That great activity planned for Q2 next year simply does not exist. In most cases, retailers have very specific launch windows that don't slip for any one branded manufacturer's plea.

This leads to . . . **the mad scramble**

- Trying to put together an innovation to hit the launch window in 25% of the original (already tight) timeline. What happens?
  - Poor product
  - Limited differentiation
  - More heavily promoted.
- Now, help me out, which three things undermine brands, profitability and consumer trust? You guessed it! Poorly performing products, products that are exactly the same as

Box 4.3: How funnels stifle innovation	
1	Focus on picking winners, not creating winners
2	'Gate' admin is at the heart, not ideas
3	Promotes 'not invented here' syndrome
4	Makes it take longer
5	Senior expertise focused on evaluation not improvement
6	Adds cost
7	Assumes good ideas are easy to come by
8	Wastes ideas
9	Demands no insight
10	Creates gaps in marketing plans

all the rest but claim to be oh-so-different and, finally, endless BOGOFFs and money-off promotions accompanying new launches.

So, it appears that funnels are a chief architect of gaps and late crises in our marketing plans, undermining our entire business plan and future growth and profitability (see Box 4.3).

We need to fix this.

A dizzying conclusion

What is happening to innovation managed by the funnel is a self-perpetuating spiral of decline. As innovation projects fail, so the requirement for accountability rises and the cycle repeats itself – (see Figure 4.8).

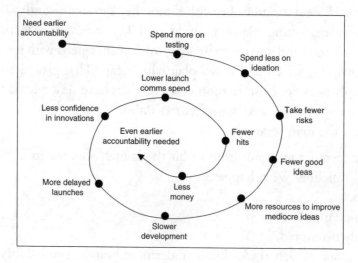

Figure 4.8: The Innovation death spiral.

This relentless pursuit of earlier innovation accountability and increased testing is getting major branded businesses nowhere. It is destroying value and wasting resources. There must be ways in which we can break out of this cycle and make the innovation process work more effectively. The spiral must be reversed so that it becomes easier to make innovation pay. It can then become a cycle of return, as in Figure 4.9.

Changing the innovation process into an innovation return cycle – where less resource is used to create more successful ideas – is the central theme of this book.

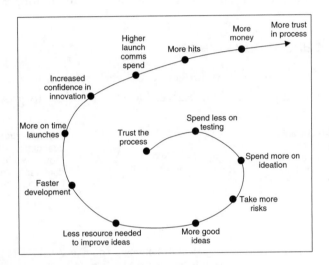

Figure 4.9: The Innovation return cycle.

We're not talking radical

This book is not going to deal specifically with radical innovation: where intention is to carve out new markets and new income streams from businesses, markets or technologies that do not lie within your core business or have yet to be invented. This topic is dealt with very expertly in many books, particularly the insightful *Blue Ocean Strategy* by W. Chan Kim and Renée Mauborgne[6]. Of course, projects tasked with creating new ideas well out of the sphere of current competence can readily use the tools, techniques and principles laid out in this book. The focus will be on core innovation – creating growth with existing brands, existing markets, and going head-to-head with tough competitors.

---

[6]W. Chan Kim & Renee Mauborgne (2005) *Blue Ocean Strategy: How to create uncontested market space and make competition irrelevant*, Harvard Business School Press

Radical out-of-the box innovation, however, does get very good press when it succeeds. It is a CEO's dream to be seen as a business pioneer, charting new oceans of opportunity. When written up in the history books the big leaps forward are those that grab all the headlines, naturally, but core innovation is harder to do.

Hey, wait a minute! How can innovating in our heartland, where our expertise lies, be tougher than inventing something totally new where we have little or no expertise, no exact data and no experience?

Once again; core innovation is harder to do than radical innovation. Why?

Between a rock and a hard place

Radical innovation (Figure 4.10) gets longer to deliver, more time and focus from senior management and more latitude to be creative. Developing ideas to grow the core of your

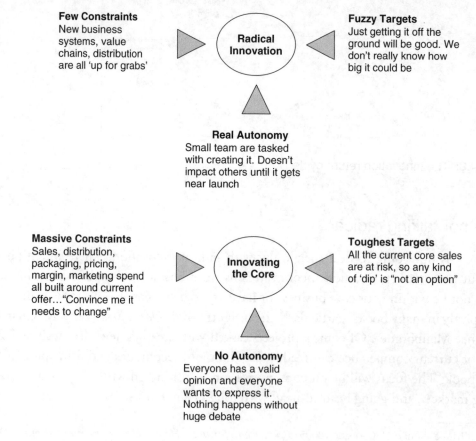

Few Constraints
New business systems, value chains, distribution are all 'up for grabs'

Radical Innovation

Fuzzy Targets
Just getting it off the ground will be good. We don't really know how big it could be

Real Autonomy
Small team are tasked with creating it. Doesn't impact others until it gets near launch

Massive Constraints
Sales, distribution, packaging, pricing, margin, marketing spend all built around current offer…"Convince me it needs to change"

Innovating the Core

Toughest Targets
All the current core sales are at risk, so any kind of 'dip' is "not an option"

No Autonomy
Everyone has a valid opinion and everyone wants to express it. Nothing happens without huge debate

Figure 4.10: Innovating the core vs. Radical innovation.

business takes on all the constraints. Marketers the world over, when tasked with innovating in their businesses heartland, know that the road ahead is very bumpy. One the one hand they have a set of competitors that know them intimately, know their customers as well as they do and pore over the same market data they do day after day looking for weaknesses to exploit and gaps to fill. On the other hand, their whole organization is set up to do things the way they are today – systems, processes, relationships, deals and factories all geared to the efficient delivery of the status quo. There are detailed sales plans, quarterly budgets, bonus schemes, 3-year strategic plans and earnings per share expectations heaped upon the performance of the core product in its core market. Everyone wants to have a say and nothing will be changed unless there is a cast iron guarantee of success. Sometimes even the best football players in the world fluff the most basic of things – the penalty kick – when they have huge expectations loaded upon them. But when they are knocking about on the practice pitch trying a radical new move, they can hit a tin can at 40 yards time and time again. When you are a top marketer charged with putting your team in front in your core market, it's really difficult. As one senior global marketer in Kraft put it to me:

> We have all these great innovation projects that we pour so much resource into all through the year. When I look back I keep thinking 'is that all we did, just a new flavour?'. It's not moving us forward but it's tiring us out.

Oat so tough

Quaker's Oat So Simple (Figure 4.11) is a good example of innovating the core. A traditional porridge breakfast cereal that was bought by older consumers in the UK harking back to a simpler age was reinvented into a thriving contemporary healthy breakfast choice by the innovation into microwaveable one-portion sachets. Sales of oats in the UK have taken off with younger health conscious consumers buying into the natural, low GI and now convenient way to set yourself up for the day. As ever, this innovation looks obvious in hindsight. But microwaves have been with us for many years and it took the switched on team at Quaker to put two and two together and come up with a winning idea that reinvigorated their core product.

Shaving close to the core

Gillette is the poster boy for core innovation. Having launched the world-beating Gillette Contour twin blade razor, and built the Gillette Series range of grooming products around it, they didn't become complacent. On the contrary, they ploughed $1 billion into developing an even better razor. Just when competitors such as Schick/Wilkinson were getting confident

Figure 4.11: Quaker's Oats So Simple.

in two-blade razors, Gillette launched the Mach 3 three-blade razor and once again reinforced its global leadership. But then when Schick/Wilkinson beat them to four-blade razors with the launch of Quattro, where were Gillette? Did they spend time and resources in uncharted waters (perhaps moving into men's grooming salons)? No. They were consolidating their position, preparing their next leapfrog innovation at home, in their core market. The launch of the Gillette Fusion has put them back in the forefront of innovation in their market. In fact, for most loyal consumers, they never left the top spot.

Obviously this blade-upmanship cannot go on indefinitely, but as a consumer I am happy to sit back and watch Gillette continually innovate their core (Figure 4.12). It all means a better shave for me!

So how is it done? How can marketers fight against the constraints of their incumbent business system? How can they drag their ideas through an innovation process and still ensure that they end up with a better chance of succeeding?

If you scan the shelves of marketing and business books you will find many tomes dedicated to the alternative to the 'innovation by numbers' approach of the funnel. They can be summarized as:

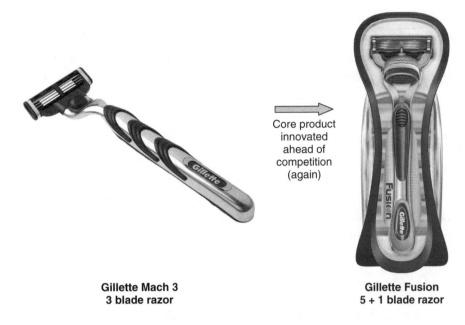

Core product
innovated
ahead of
competition
(again)

Gillette Mach 3
3 blade razor

Gillette Fusion
5 + 1 blade razor

Figure 4.12: Gillette's core innovation.

Be a Rebel!

'Be like the business mega-stars and found your own maverick dynasty' is the attractive offer. Prime pin-up rebels are people likes of Steve Jobs of Apple, Richard Branson of Virgin and Jeff Bezos of Amazon. Each one has built a business empire from the ground up, breaking all the rules and never taking 'no' for an answer. Theirs is a particular DNA that marked them out from the word go.

If, like them, you happen to be a CEO, starting your own company or a billionaire, then go ahead and follow the rebel mantra:

- Go to work prepared to lose your job every day
- Unleash your inner creativity at every opportunity
- Don't just challenge conventions, ignore **all** constraints
- Do things differently, very differently.
- Be a pirate, gather a band of like-minded cut-throats and pledge allegiance to the relentless pursuit of your vision.

Although this approach may be fun, it is simply not relevant for most marketers in major branded businesses. They are not solely in charge of their own destinies, CEOs charting a course through Blue Oceans of opportunity or wealthy loners looking for something to put their money into. Today's marketers are sharp eyed, smart thinking modern businessmen and women who know that if they leverage the vast resources of their companies correctly, they can unleash revolutionary growth, change the world and still have fun. That way they will rise through the ranks, not destroy them.

The choice

So is this the choice we have as innovators: to be funnel monkeys, filling the admin coffers with endless reports, trying to turn ideas into business winners by throwing more and more data at them, or to thumb our nose at our organization and break all the rules, the chairs and probably the bank, in upheaving everything to get to our Nirvana of newness?

There must be a better way

There must be a path that gives us the best of both worlds – as inspirational and exciting as being a rebel, but as accountable and predictable as a perfect funnel should be (Figure 4.13).

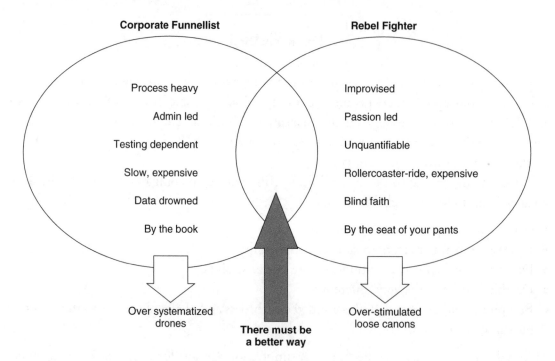

Figure 4.13: The two sides of the innovation process.

Key takeouts

1 Innovation is the key growth strategy of our age (so we had better be good at it).
2 Growing core brands in their core markets is harder than radical innovation as it carries the weight of the whole company with every move.
3 A strong desire for accountability and objective measurement leads to admin outweighing creativity in the innovation process.
4 Good-quality ideas are not easy to come by, and testing them more does not improve them.
5 Funnels are stifling innovation.
6 Being a rebel only works for CEOs or maverick misfits, not for most marketers.
7 There must be a better way to develop ideas.

Checklist: Is innovation being stifled by your funnel?

Stifle-O-Meter

	Yes	No
• Do the stage-gate processes (presentations, meetings, justification) take up more time and effort than was spent creating and crafting the ideas?	☐	☐
• Does your funnel contain similar, competing concepts/projects from different regions because 'our market is different'?	☐	☐
• Do senior managers spend more time evaluating than building ideas?	☐	☐
• Do you think you could achieve the same results with less cost (on evaluation)?	☐	☐
• Do you think you could achieve the same (or better) results faster?	☐	☐
• Do you look at the funnel and feel it is full of too many low quality ideas?	☐	☐
• Do ideas/concepts that failed along the way get discarded completely?	☐	☐
• Do innovations often slip leaving you with awkward gaps in marketing plans?	☐	☐
Totals	☐ :	☐

Handover

Consider yourself fully briefed on the reasons why this book has been written. We've seen how funnels are stifling innovation and just how important it is that branded businesses look for a new way to develop their ideas. So sit back and strap yourself in. You're about to take a rocket ride.

The Core Idea

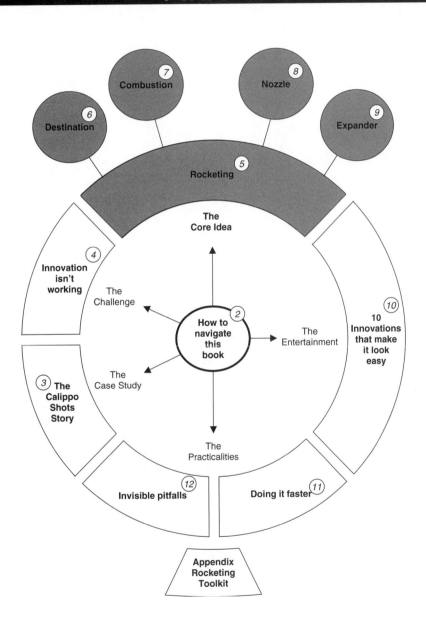

PART III

A new innovation paradigm: The Rocket Motor

 Headlines

Introducing a new paradigm for innovation – the rocket motor. Based on the principles of how a real rocket motor works, this is a powerful new way to design and run innovation processes. The four constituent parts are headlined: Destination (having a clear vision),

Combustion (generating high quality ideas), Nozzle (quickly getting to the strongest ideas), Expander (building them into winning mixes).

Innovation is, in fact, Rocket science

So, if funnels are stifling innovation, what can we replace them with? This chapter introduces the new paradigm of

A Rocket Motor

as the successor to the innovation funnel.

Rocket motors are actually very simple, not nearly as complex as internal combustion engines or jet engines. They are, in effect, controlled explosions. This is a potent paradigm for innovation, and when interrogated further, it turns into a useful evolution of the innovation funnel, containing all the key steps in an evolved innovation process, and laying out some new principles and tools.

So, contrary to hoards of wise-cracking marketers, we are about to find that innovation is, in fact, rocket science.

Boffin warning!

We are about to do some physics. Marketers of a nervous disposition when dealing with mathematical pursuits should skip to the next section. All linguists, obviously, are to look away now.

Rocket overview

Rocket motors use simple but potent fuel (liquid oxygen/liquid hydrogen) to generate vast amounts of energy (thrust) to lift themselves, and the heavy rockets they are attached to, up and out of the earth's atmosphere → *from simple inputs comes an outsized effect that lifts the entire parent structure up and out of the gravitational field that holds it down.*

This is the job innovation is intended to do for brands and businesses.

Moon shot

Figure 5.1 shows the rocket motor that powered the Saturn rockets. Six were used in the second stage of the Saturn 1 rocket, which carried the Apollo spacecraft (Figure 5.2) in the programme that put Neil Armstrong on the moon.

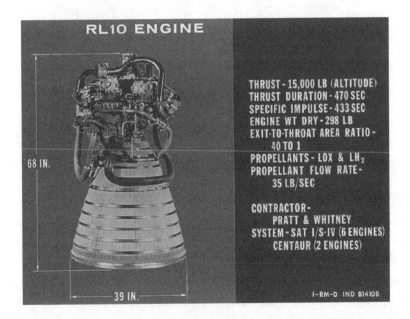

Figure 5.1: NASA's first liquid hydrogen rocket motor, 1958.

Figure 5.2: The Apollo/Saturn, NASA 1967.

So, how do rocket motors work,

Isaac Newton said "for every action there is an equal and opposite reaction" – his third (but arguably most famous) law of motion – and a rocket motor works on this simple principle (see Figure 5.3).

Fuels are combined in a combustion chamber where they create huge volumes of hot gases which escape through a small nozzle at very high velocities. Thrust is the reaction on the motor structure in opposition to the exhaust gases leaving so quickly. This is the same force that pushes a garden hose backward as the water squirts out.

Destination

Designers of rocket motors define the overall size and key ratios between the various chambers according to the rocket's destination. Mission control gives a clear picture of the pressures, temperatures and requirements of the atmosphere in which the rocket will be used. The

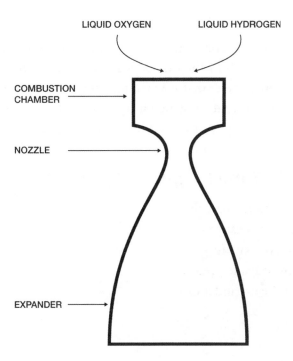

Figure 5.3: How a rocket motor works.

motor is then designed to work optimally in those conditions. This is why space rockets have at least two stages: one motor works best in the Earths' atmosphere (stage 1), the next in near space (stage 2) and finally, if there is landing craft, it has a third motor that works best in the Moon's atmosphere.

Combustion chamber

The combustion chamber is where the fuels are burned at high pressure. The combustion chamber typically has to withstand up to 250 times standard air pressure and temperatures of up to 3600°C.

Nozzle

The nozzle is there to convert all the heat and pressure in the combustion chamber into kinetic energy – movement. It converts the slow-moving, high-pressure, high-temperature gas into fast-moving, lower pressure, cooler gas – like air coming out of a balloon.

As we all learned at school: Force = Mass × Acceleration. So a very high acceleration for the mass of gas produces a very big force.

Expander

As the hot exhaust gases travel along the expander, they are expanding and getting lower in pressure accordingly. The job of the expander is to deliver them at the exit at the same pressure as the outside atmosphere; that is when maximum thrust is achieved. An expander is therefore designed for the altitude at which it has to operate.

If this is written as an equation (just for the fun of it!) we get:

$$\textbf{\textit{Thrust} = \textit{qV}_e + (\textit{P}_e - \textit{P}_a)\,\textit{A}_e}$$

where: q = rate of exhaust mass flow
V_e = speed of exhaust gases
P_e = pressure of exhaust gases
P_a = ambient/outside pressure
A_e = area of the expander exit.

Everyone got that?

Enough rocket science – get with the innovation

If we convert the core elements of a rocket motor into innovation steps, we find a new paradigm for innovation (see Figure 5.4).

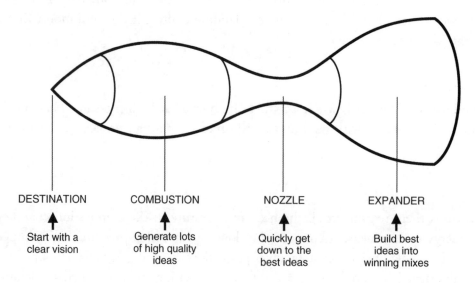

Figure 5.4: The Innovation Rocket.

Rather than a funnel shape that starts empty, attracts random inputs and attempts to squeeze out a few drops of innovation at the end, we have a rocket with a clear destination, creating ideas as it goes and focused on producing maximum impact from the resources we put in. The key constituent parts are listed below.

Destination

Being clear on where you are going, what your goal is, is the first and crucial step in successful innovation. Here are three key elements:

- *Clear vision*: Starting with a clear vision of where you want to end up together with strong direction from the brand and its core value drivers, and building them in as the first step of the innovation process, greatly improves efficiency and the likelihood of generating ideas that deliver. The Rocket paradigm creates ideas within the framework of a clear destination.
- *Design the process with the end in mind*: The whole design of the innovation process itself is dictated by the end goal. Why use cookie-cutter processes with slight tweaks in order to meet a range of entirely different innovation challenges? The scope of the opportunity, the urgency to deliver, the personnel involved and the competitive context must all dictate the design of the process.
- *Map tomorrow*: The third key aspect of defining your destination is that it forces the team to consider the end point. This means modelling what the context will be when your innovation comes to market – with changes in competition, distribution and consumer behaviour according to trends. No rocket ever made it to the Moon by considering only the lunar position at time of lift off. Building in a Destination step forces you to build innovations for the way you expect the market to be.

Combustion

Thinking about the idea generation process as a continuous combustion process is a powerful metaphor. It insists on the following things:

- *Continuous insight fuel*: Does the research that you commission act as potent fuel for ideation? Seeing insight as a vital component of an explosion drives you to dig deeper, go broader and take more risks with your insight inputs. This is what is needed to ensure that the most incendiary idea generation comes out of it.
- *Multiple ignition process*: Turning continuous insight into a healthy stream of high-quality ideas needs more than just a standard brainstorming session. Multiple simultaneous ideation sessions with different styles, techniques and outputs dramatically increase the quality and quantity of ideas created.

- *3 Bucket Principle*: With so many more ideas around it is vital that they are managed effectively. Not an accounting package but a potent simple method for sorting, retaining and recycling ideas. Never ditch an idea, however odd it seems, as there may be value in it someway down the track. The three buckets helps you get the most from your ideas.

Nozzle

The nozzle is the heart of the new innovation process and unleashes time and resource into the rest of the process in three ways:

- *Theatre rules*: Taking cues from showbusiness can dramatically change the way you do all your innovation meetings for the better. Performing ideas, telling stories and bringing ideas to life is much more fruitful (and fun) than allowing them to get lost in endless PowerPoint. New ideas are very vulnerable and are unable to fend for themselves in large organizations.
- *Swift prioritization*: A huge amount of time and resource is piled into evaluation and whittling down ideas to a 'winner' that could much more profitably be used elsewhere in the process. The key to unleashing this is swift prioritization of ideas – using simple techniques and strong deadlines to agree on the most promising ideas quickly.
- *Objective evaluation*: Using a set of agreed evaluation criteria to capture all feedback on new ideas is a simple but highly effective way of getting the clarity of objectivity into innovation decision making. It speeds up decisions and helps to avoid internal politics from derailing projects.

Expander

This is where ideas are turned into launch-ready products and services. This shortcuts the standard go-to-market process by building the idea into a mix much earlier.

- *Building/expanding ideas*: The priority is to stop the evaluation after the nozzle stage, and focus all energy and resource on making the idea bigger and better. Few (if any) ideas are born whole as complete mixes. They need to grow and fill out and very often only begin to become really powerful when they have other ideas built in across different parts of the mix.
- *360° mix development*: Rather than just developing and refining a concept to 'pass' a hurdle, the Expander process looks at the full mix. It takes the principle of prototyping to the next logical step, developing an idea across the full 360° spectrum of the mix. Sometimes the best ideas only come to life when added to by some other seemingly less important part of the mix, such as new secondary packaging or a different communication

channel. The aim is to achieve the optimum impact at launch, rather than at the next stage-gate.

- *Better use of senior expertise*: As we have seen in the funnel innovation process, the most senior and experienced resource is used almost exclusively to evaluate ideas and point out failings. In the Innovation Rocket this is turned on its head so that the most senior people focus on building ideas, adding to them and solving problems in order to maximize impact.

Maximizing impact

In rocket motors the maximum thrust you can get is when the expander has worked so efficiently that the gases are at the same pressure as the outsider atmosphere when they leave. That means that all their energy has been converted into thrust.

This same principle can be applied to the Innovation Rocket: an idea will have maximum impact when it has been expanded and developed in all dimensions of the mix to such an extent that it fits perfectly into the market space it was intended for and retailers grab it with both hands.

This is the role that the local markets should be playing when rolling out multi-market or global innovations. Rather than argue over the brands or design, their effort should be focused on creating maximum thrust: 'How can we add to the idea by developing a new part of the mix for maximum impact in our market' should be the mantra. It represents a sure but powerful perception shift for receiving markets:

From:	*To:*
Making it **fit** my market	Maximizing the **impact**
Implication:	*Implication:*
• What should we change? • What won't work?	• What can I add? • How can I make it work?

Stand well back

Once you have lit the Innovation Rocket, it's time to stand well back – as it says on every box of fireworks. It should produce a lot of heat and noise and needs to find its own equilibrium.

Don't interfere too much with the inner workings of the combustion process, just watch for what is coming out. Teams need to be allowed to disappear while they truly absorb themselves in innovation at the early stages.

Skunk working

In the glory days of aircraft design and manufacturing–when governments were handing out large contracts for fighter and bomber aircraft on a regular basis–the American defence industries defined the process of 'skunk working' to solve the challenges that were needed to develop the next generation of aircraft. This entailed choosing a project leader and letting that person gather a small band of like-minded individuals from across the different departments and sending them down to the other end of the runway to a small workshop. They remained there until they had resolved the essentials of the challenge they had been given. They had open access to any technology in the business and, more critically, they were left alone. No senior management involvement, no status reviews, no lengthy approvals – just an expectation of specific results within a clear timeframe. This process proved highly successful in creating breakthroughs such as the Stealth Bomber.

This is a very good analogy for the Rocketing style of innovation:

- Having an unequivocal end goal with an immovable deadline
- Giving teams plenty of space to generate their ideas in many different ways using multiple sources of inspiration and experience
- Taking decisions and prioritizing ideas swiftly, without political interference
- Focusing much more energy and time on building ideas and solving problems than picking faults and formal tests.

Key takeouts

1 There is a powerful new paradigm for innovation: the Rocket Motor
2 It has four constituents parts:
    - Destination – Defining a clear goal as the first critical step
    - Combustion – Continuous high-quality idea generation
    - Nozzle – Swift prioritization of ideas
    - Expander – Building maximum impact mixes.
3 It is an evolution of the funnel, but focuses more on building ideas and solving problems than on whittling down to a 'winner'.
4 Innovation is, in fact, rocket science.

 **Handover**

Now that we have seen a new paradigm for innovation to replace the funnel, we'll go through the next four workouts in detail to explain each part and how you can work with it.

Rocketing: Destination

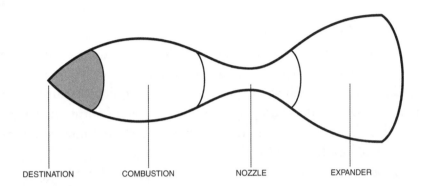

CHAPTER 6

DESTINATION   COMBUSTION   NOZZLE   EXPANDER

 ## Headlines

Having a clear vision is the critical first step to successful innovation. Make sure it delivers on your brand vision and is writ large on your team's minds, so that they have a collectively clear vision of the end point, otherwise it's too easy to end up hamster-wheeling – going round and round getting nowhere. Galvanize your decision making and project efficiency by turning target dates into sharp do-or-die 'drop-dead' lines. Above all, begin with the end in mind.

Being clear

The first part of the Rocketing approach to innovation is to be clear on your destination. Even though the precise answer is a mystery (or at least unclear), it doesn't mean that your vision of what the innovation should achieve need be fuzzy. The clearer you are about the end result – what it must achieve, and for whom and how – the better. How you set about defining your vision and the quality of what you come up with is vital for a successful project, and ultimately a successful new innovation.

Use your brand

The first port of call for any marketer in defining the vision for an innovation is the brand. Your brand positioning should give you clear direction on what you need to deliver with your innovations to fulfil your brand's vision. This topic is extensively covered in the brandgym books *Brand Stretch*[1] and *Brand Vision*.[2] A good example is the Pampers brand.

Pampers: a clear vision for innovation

After 40 years focused on nappies (diapers) and dryness protection, the Pampers team developed a bigger, bolder vision at the end of the 1990s. This new vision (see Figure 6.1 for my colleague David Taylor's stab at the masterbrand positioning) has inspired and guided a transformation of the product range as well as new communication. Upgrades of the core nappy range have boosted share in the UK by over 10% and innovation into adjacent markets has added on new business worth over $150 million.

This new positioning avoided the risk with masterbrands of a strategy that is fat and flabby in an attempt to cover off every possible product extension. Pampers took a clear and confident stance in focusing on child development. This helped the positioning to perform well against the key criteria for a brand vision that will drive strong innovation:

- *Motivating*: The promise of giving you the confidence to care for your baby's development was a big idea with an emotional component. This not only made it motivating for consumers, but also inspiring for the brand team. However, this promise was underpinned by a clear functional *benefit* of 'healthy skin = happy baby able to play, learn and develop'. In other words, there was some sausage and not just sizzle.
- *Different*: The emphasis on child development was very different to the more light-hearted and playful positioning of key competitor Huggies. It had a further advantage of being hard to copy by less expert retailer own-label diaper brands.
- *True*: The positioning was supported by some clear product *truths* via high-performance products. The basic 'Baby Dry' diaper range already provided superior dryness protection. In addition, innovative new brand extensions were essential to really dramatizing the new vision.

---

[1]Taylor, D. (2004) *Brand Stretch: Why 1 in 2 Extensions Fail and How to Beat the Odds.* John Wiley & Sons.
[2]Taylor, D. (2007) *Brand Vision: How to energize your team to drive business growth.* John Wiley & Sons.

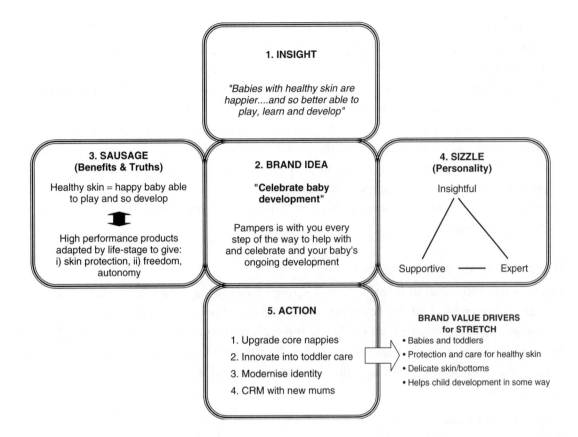

Figure 6.1: Pampers Masterbrand Vision.

Bottom-up innovation

Innovation translated the Pampers promise into new products that did more to help parents to care for their young children's delicate skin. The bigger and bolder vision inspired and guided not only the upgrading of the core business but also innovation into new areas that would have been less likely with the old, dryness focused positioning:

- *Upgrade core nappy business*: A new range of premium-priced diapers was designed to meet the needs of babies at different stages of development. For example, 'New Baby' was specially developed for (ugh) 'runny poo' that comes from a liquid diet. 'Active Fit' has extra stretchy sides to provide a perfect fit when the baby is older and on the move (they crawl up to a quarter of a mile in 20 minutes; no wonder parents are continually worn out). These new extensions clearly dramatized the brand's understanding of baby development *and* the use of this in developing products. In the 18 months following the 2001 relaunch, market share grew strongly from 47% to 55%, driven by the premium-priced new innovations.

- *Innovate into toddler care*: Kandoo is a moist and flushable toilet wipe in an impactful and easy-to-use dispenser. Again, this is great manifestation of the brand's baby development promise, by helping young children to gain independence in their attempts to use the 'big toilet'. The product is supported by the brand's product benefit of cleaning and caring for skin. This innovation has exceeded all sales targets and the product has how a four-fold position over its nearest competitor, Johnson & Johnson Extra Clean. Along with the existing baby wipes innovations, this new business has provided over $150 million of incremental business.

Remember what made you famous

Pampers has succeeded in using innovation to go from being a product brand focused on dryness to become a child development specialist focused on baby care. Defining a series of *'brand value drivers'* can help to guide the type of innovation an which your brand could focus. One way to generate these drivers is to ask yourself 'What made us famous in the first place?' and 'What is really driving value for our consumers?. For Pampers this could lead to the following:

1 Babies and toddlers
2 Protection and care for healthy skin
3 Delicate skin/bottoms
4 Help in at least a small way child development

Pampers summary

1 An insight-based single-minded positioning
2 Innovation from clear product truths
3 Ask what made you famous and use the answer to guide innovation efforts

---

Hamster-wheeling

Too often projects start because 'we need an innovation for Q2' and no one ever defines the end result more clearly than that. The ensuing project is then set up to be a fraught, resource-draining fight to the bitter end. And to what end? Innovation projects often just keep rebooting themselves and moving off in new directions because no one was really clear at the start where they were headed. What are the signs that you don't have a clear enough destination? Hamster-wheeling.

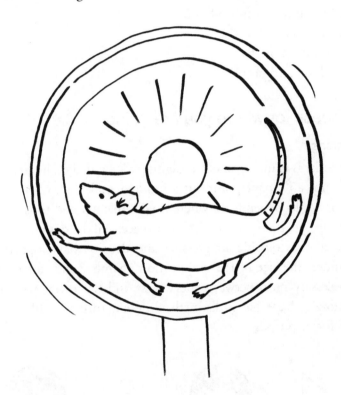

Do you ever get the feeling in the middle of an innovation project that you've been here before? That all these issues and ideas that are being created have already been created in some previous project? Welcome to innovation hamster-wheeling – going on and on but never actually getting anywhere. This is an affliction that affects many innovation projects and is caused by the lack of a clearly defined vision. The team are keenly pursuing every avenue, but without a shared end result in each of their heads, the issues just go round and round.

Begin with the end in mind

The guiding principle with which to tackle this is: Start with the end in mind. Like a great tennis player, who visualizes where the ball will land before it is hit, you and your team need to de clear on your destination before you even contemplate an ideas quest.

There are six key aspects of beginning with the end in mind, they are:

- Design the process for where you are going
- Get a clear vision of the end result
- Turn your deadlines into 'drop-dead' lines
- Map tomorrow, not today
- Write a good innovation brief
- Paint your vision loud and proud.

Design the process for where you are going

A rocket motor analogy

When a rocket scientist is thinking about designing a new rocket, he first must know where it is going. This is not a flippant point but a fundamental piece of rocket design, because how a rocket motor works depends on where it will operate, and thus its destination. Two motors intended to propel their craft to different places will be designed differently.

External factors, such as outside air pressure and density, have a great influence on the shape of the expander, the size of the combustion chamber and, for maximum efficiency and thrust, the necessary ratio between the widest and narrowest parts of the nozzle. In Figure 6.2, each nozzle shape has a distinctly different thrust profile; thus each motor is uniquely designed for its purpose.

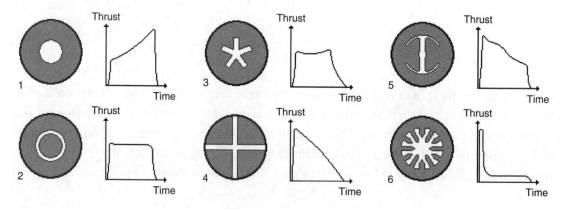

Figure 6.2: Cross-section of nozzles from different rocket motors.

This principle holds true for innovation process design.

How you get there depends on where you're going

Too often teams use the same innovation process to solve very different problems and then wonder why they find it difficult to succeed. When devising a totally new brand platform, it cannot be right to use the same process that was used to invent the new flavour for the summer sales promotion. Yet time and again the same process is used across all manner of problems.

Factors influencing your process design

There are four key factors to consider when designing your next innovation project (see Table 6.1):

1 *Speed*: How quickly do you need the answer? Define your end deliverable and exact format and work back to give you a time frame. Faster projects require different techniques like

Table 6.1: Factors influencing process design.

Speed is paramount	SPEED	More relaxed timelines
• Process steps in parallel • Real time inputs from experts in workshops • Longer workshops with evening consumer input • On the spot design		• Inputs from multiple sources; experts from all markets • Multiple shorter workshops with time to 'noodle' in between • Use a design agency to add real thought & value
Tight Focus	**BANDWIDTH**	**Broad scope**
• Fresh, diverse inputs • Different teams approaching the same problem • Express ideas in different formats: drawings, longhand descriptions, etc.		• Get insight and inputs across the full spectrum • Divide areas up amongst the team • Build in moments when focus is narrowed and choices are made
Senior stakeholders	**WHO'S INVOLVED**	**Regional/local teams**
• Hold separate brainstorming sessions for senior input • Do regular one-on-one feedback sessions • Capture senior comments in an Idea Power matrix – not in front of the whole team		• Parallel brainstorming sessions in each local market, then pooling ideas • Update calls to local markets after significant workshops • Put key dates in diaries at the start – then have an open invitation
Concept test	**MILESTONE FORMAT**	**Big presentation**
• Plan a quick and dirty online test before full test • Brief copywriters to perfect your ideas in real consumer speak		• Brief agencies to create 3D mock-ups and 'stuff' • Plan in time to rehearse

'hot' consumer recycling. Slower, longer projects can use more sequential steps and take advantage of more and varied inputs. Use your time to get inspired by different processes that stretch and challenge you. Above all, a fast project should not just mean 'do it quick' (and thus shoddily), nor should a slower project mean 'take your time' (i.e. lose focus and energy).

2 *Bandwidth*: How many ideas do you want to create? Across how many categories? These are vital questions in the briefing of an innovation task and are too often left open and vague. To create a huge amount of good ideas at the end (10 or more) you need huge quantities of insight 'fuel' and a big combustion/brainstorming phase. Too often teams just create more and more ideas using the same inputs and the results are, unsurprisingly, the same. The quality of most of the ideas is thus poor. Equally, with a narrow focus on the particular area where ideas are needed, having too little new input (or even none at all) leads to only having a few ideas, which greatly reduces your chances of success. When considering a broad number of territories it is often best to carve up the areas and address them separately, but still within the same team and overall process. Building in moments when you focus on only one thing at a time helps to avoid 'idea sprawl'. Much like 'urban sprawl' this phenomenon can get quite ugly. It occurs when you tackle too may targets at once in a single brainstorm session – concepts and ideas of all shapes and sizes come out, clumping together in a disjointed way and offering no overall shape that the team can grasp. This means that you get overly diverse ideas, none of which feels at home in your project.

3 *Who's involved*: Who really needs to be involved in your project? This is a critical factor that is often overlooked for the success of many projects. Involving people implicated in the outputs is a very good way of increasing your chances of success. The flipside of this is obviously that if you involve too many people then the project can grind slowly to a halt, having achieved nothing. Either way, designing your process with key stakeholders in mind is a very good discipline. Building in a specific stage where international teams can be part of the process can reap rewards – even if one brainstorming session is all the input they get, keen marketers from far flung markets will feel much more ownership for the results if they know their ideas were included. Often just planning the project far enough in advance, with dates for debriefs and key workshops fixed months ahead, will solve the involvement problem as local markets can either properly plan their trips or feel that they were given the genuine option to be involved. Calling the Venezuelan team and saying 'Can you come to the research debrief in Paris next week?' does not constitute good global involvement. The other way to get global teams involved is to plan for update calls after key events. A one-on-one call that is timely can cover a lot of ground. When dealing

with senior stakeholders who are very hands on it is smart to design the process to enable them to feel that they are involved – without compromising the project or undermining the team responsible for it. Build in a specific brainstorming session with your senior stakeholders – hold it with a small team somewhere funky and they will feel that are 'really doing it', even if you have a separate, large-scale brainstorming planned elsewhere. Using Idea Power matrices to capture their evaluation of the ideas, one-on-one enables you to get their valuable input without derailing the whole project (see Chapter 9 for details).

4 *Milestone format*: What kind of milestones are there along the way? Who is the audience for your concepts and in which situations? Starting with the end in mind is a good discipline in all endeavours, and innovation projects are no different. If your end point is a quantitative concept test where you have to beat a critical benchmark, then make sure you build in enough time to copyright the final concept and get it properly translated. You may even need to build in a quick dummy run piece of internet research to make sure your concepts are actually communicating what you want them to. Getting to the end of an expensive and exhaustive multi-market concept test and then saying 'But they didn't understand the concept properly' will not win you any innovation awards. If, on the other hand, your key milestone is a presentation to the board or a global team of senior stakeholders, and your intention is for them to give you and your idea a standing ovation, build in time and budget to create a real **performance**. Brief your design agency, buy costumes, hire props – whatever you need to create an Oscar winning performance should be planned in at the start.

Get a clear vision of the end result

Having a clear vision is a very important starting point for all innovation projects. Knowing clearly where you are headed and what the success criteria really are is a critical factor in delivering ideas that succeed (Figure 6.3). Over 90% of marketing directors in our survey agreed.

Don't accept less, **demand** a clear vision

It is probably not wrong to say that you should not embark on an innovation project without a clear vision. Whoever is responsible for the project should demand one from their seniors. Challenge your team: Is my vision clear? Does the team have a vivid mental picture of the task? This is the purpose of doing stakeholder interviews at the start of major projects. Very often barriers that were assumed to be insurmountable simply evaporate when you ask senior stakeholders directly about the scope of an innovation brief.

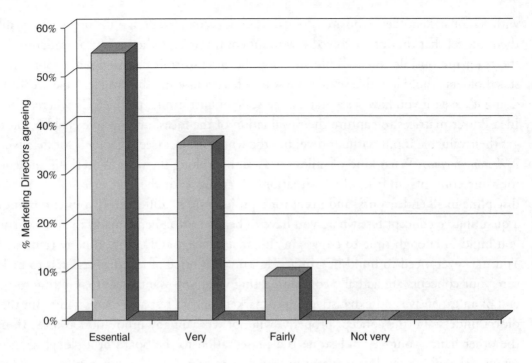

Figure 6.3: Importance of a clear innovation destination.

Source: Brandgym research.

The clearer and tighter the innovation vision, the more lateral and creative you are forced to be in seeking solutions. This is no different from briefing an advertising or design agency. The tighter the brief, the more creative the response.

To achieve great creative leaps, your brief should include the seemingly impossible, very clearly and concisely.

Turn your deadlines into 'drop-dead' lines

Your innovation project started with a bang – loads of enthusiasm and everyone involved and engaged. It peaked at the brainstorm day where everyone had fun and things seemed to be going so well. But from then on the energy and vitality seeped out of the project until only the cold hard light of day was left for the quantitative test results and the R&D verdict of 'no can do'.

It's so easy for projects to lose momentum. They can start out with all the right intentions and process steps, yet still fail. It is very likely that because decisions weren't made, at key steps in the process, delays crept in easily as approval was sought from an array of senior stakeholders. None of their input was wrong and all intended to drive a successful outcome of course, but the net result was a delayed project with the team doubting their own ability to deliver results.

This is not just about finding a more fun team, this is endemic to the process – projects that lose momentum drain life out of a team and also therefore out of the ideas it creates. To keep the energy up, you need to energize the process, not just eat more chocolate.

Introducing new, improved 'drop-dead' lines

Use your project milestones as strategic tools to galvanize innovation. They can work wonders not just in timing but in the quality and success of the overall project. Turn your ordinary deadlines into immovable, unavoidable 'drop-dead' lines. To put it another way, be a bit more like Apple.

How does Apple manage to innovate so consistently and quickly? After the triumph of the iPod, most companies would have taken two or three years to develop a range extension that would match up to the original and get it through to launch. It would have teen tested endlessly and pored over by everyone including the chairman to make sure it was just right, making a quick launch impossible.

Mac World: Apple's secret weapon

Apple have a huge advantage over almost everyone – it's called Mac World Expo. This huge yearly public show is their own 'drop-dead' line. When Steve Jobs stands up in front of the world to make one of his famous virtuoso two-hour speeches, the product is most definitely ready to go. He is not going to stand up and say: "We had a problem in testing so we pushed the programme back, it should be available in two months." That is not the way things work at Apple. Steve Jobs has created a super high profile: must deliver, no excuses, do or die deadline that every single person in his organization knows about, right down to the sandwich delivery guy. *That's a 'drop-dead' line.* It works wonders.

Benefits of drop-dead lines

- *Increases creativity*: There's nothing like a deadline to focus the creative mind. From comedians to writers, artists and wartime mathematicians, having an immovable looming deadline has spurred some of the finest leaps of creativity around.
- *Forces ingenious solutions*: The simple phase 'needs must' sums this up. When faced with a problem, a serious deadline (often impending peril) forces us to explore new avenues to find solutions. Every James Bond film is packed with such things – from snowboarding with a broken skidoo ski (*Moonraker*) to freefalling off a mountaintop to catch a falling plane (*Goldeneye*). A little bit of 007 would do every innovation project some good!

- *Creates priorities*: That critical innovation meeting that usually takes ages to set up because of people's diary clashes, suddenly becomes top priority when everyone can feel the impending 'drop-dead' line. "Can we move it back a month, my schedule is packed" becomes "What time tomorrow?"
- *Forces decisions*: One of the things that weighs innovation down is the series of tough decisions that have to be made; which brand should it go under, what will the name be, do we go with one SKU or two at launch? Decisions that usually result in lengthy deliberations, seeking of permissions, budget processes, etc., suddenly are made there and then. They are not taken lightly or flippantly, but they are taken and the team moves on. 'Drop-dead' lines don't wait for ditherers.

'Drop-Dead' lines = Red Bull for Innovation

- *Prevents gaps appearing in your Innovation Roadmap*: How many times in projects does a problem occur and the immediate response is to slip the timeline in order to fix the problem? Suddenly your nicely laid out innovation plan has a gap in Q4 as everything has slipped by six months. Multiply this by several innovation projects across several brands and you have the continual chaos that clogs up the management time in most major FMCG multinationals. 'Drop-dead' lines get more projects to deliver on time. That means fewer gaps.

Powerade: first off the blocks

Back in the 1990s the European sports drink market was in a strong growth phase. No one brand owned the space. In the UK Lucozade and Lucozade Sport were big, but there was room for more big players. The Coca-Cola company had been eyeing this opportunity but had not made a move. It had Powerade in the USA and Australia, but nothing in the UK and different offers across Europe.

One day Coke got wind that Gatorade, the market leader in the USA, was due to launch in the UK in three months' time. This was their 'drop-dead' line.

The Powerade challenge

Deliver a full mix sports drink for the UK (and Europe) ready to go immediately into full production in 90 days

---

That meant 60 days to find the most relevant and differentiated proposition, full artwork for a European audience and a workable pack structure. The team was small and reported straight to the top. The innovation process itself was innovated: working with Added Value, the team created a totally new process that would develop the proposition, pack design and product simultaneously using consumers continuously, not just in lengthy qualitative studies.

They used unorthodox creatives, rough and ready insight techniques with both core and fringe consumers. They focused on the UK only, using expertise and experience within the company to check for European compatibility. They took on a scavenger attitude, going through every pack and product in the vast European Coca-Cola business. The team delivered in 60 days. The final pack was from a small sports water brand in Austria. The design was the US version – it didn't cause any problems with European consumers so why change it? The flavours were new, but from well-known available ingredients and within comfortable manufacturing parameters. The proposition was fine tuned in situ to deliver just what the European sporty teen and twenty-something wanted: 100% energy, 100% of the time.

Powerade launched on time in the UK and ahead of Gatorade. This secured a strong start to what is now a very significant pan-European brand, Gatorade was stymied.

Powerade summary

1 Crystal clear irreversible deadline
2 Begged, borrowed or stole with pride
3 Reinvented the inventing process to fit the task

Map tomorrow, not today

Good footballers move to where the ball is. Great footballers move to where the ball will be. This is the same for great innovators; they anticipate market needs and arrive at just the right moment. Too many innovation briefs assume that the world stays just as it is, that everything is in stasis just waiting for your dazzling idea to burst upon the scene. This is patently not the case – the world continues to boil and bubble, new ideas from all quarters arriving every moment and old ones dying off. This constant change needs to be considered when defining your vision for innovation and thus for each and every specific brief.

Segment for tomorrow

The best way to tackle this is to reconsider your market segmentation. This topic deserves a book on its own as it is a fundamental piece of all marketing strategy. In this instance we

Table 6.2: European soft drink market year 2000: Product segmentation. (*Source:* Author's experience).

Segments	Product							
	Soft drinks Still	Soft drinks: carbonated	Water: bottled	Energy drinks	Squash/dilutes	Kids' drinks	Fruit juices	Iced tea
Vol/value	Medium	Very large	Large	Low	Medium	Medium	Large	Medium
Growth	High	Low	High	Medium	Low	Medium	High	Medium
Formats	Singles	Singles Multi-packs Large bottles	Singles Large bottles Multi-packs	Singles Multi-packs	1 litre bottles	Singles	1 litre cartons singles	Singles Large bottles
Target	Teens/young adults	Teens and broad	Families Women	Young men	Families	Families	Families	Teens Families
Needs	Refreshment and snacking	Refreshment and snacking	Refreshment and detox	Energy	Refreshment	Fun and refreshment	Refreshment and health	Refreshment and health

will look at it from the point of view of laying the foundation for successful innovation. This can be achieved in two steps:

1 *Change how your market is segmented* to twist it in your favour. This need not be a major exercise with quantitative validation (although this is a very good idea if you are embarking on a major new series of brand-changing innovations). It can be developed as a hypothesis among the team to open new areas of opportunity.
2 *Stretch the new axes into the future* by using trends analysis to give you direction and pace of change. Again this need not be a major quantitative exercise, but a stimulating way to look at the drivers of culture and how they are evolving, then applying these to the dimensions of your market and seeing how it reshapes as these drivers take hold.

For example – Innovating Soft Drinks in Europe: If we take the European soft drinks market in 2000 as our starting point, we can see how this technique can yield very fertile ground for innovation. A typical product-based segmentation might well have looked like the one in Table 6.2.

There is nothing wrong with this kind of segmentation – it is correct. It's just that it's not very insightful. Any player in the market or new entrant, however small, could gather this kind of segmentation information very readily. All players are therefore looking at the same opportunities, as shown in Box 6.1.

I am sure that some good marketers are reading this that have toiled away on such fruitless projects. Certainly the shelves have been full of such innovations over the last six years, most of which have disappeared without a trace. Were the innovations wrong? No – they didn't stand a chance from the moment the uninspired brief was written. Getting a good brief is a huge 'leg up' for any innovation – and by 'good' that means it contains an insight into the market of the future. The Calippo shots brief 'saw' a world where teens didn't reject all water-ices. Renault 'saw' a world where families were comfortable and had what they wanted to hand on their journey when they briefed the Scenic.

Let's look again at the same market, but this time let's segment from a different point of view – not rigidly by needs or consumer groups, but by opportunity segments that we identify just by observing the market and looking at the joins, the discontinuities and what is emerging. The result is a very different map of the market. It is much harder to quantify. The sizes of these segments do not just fall out of a standard tracker study. But that is not the purpose of this segmentation; the aim is to **write better innovation briefs**.

Box 6.1: Common opportunities

Opportunities emerging	Resulting innovations
• Get into bottled water ⟶	A.N. Other Natural Spring
• Do more still drinks ⟶	Endless new flavours
• Do a kid's version ⟶	Cartoon character on carton
• Get into energy drinks ⟶	Ultra-niche 'cool' drink

Table 6.3: European Soft Drinks Market 2000: Innovation segmentation. (*Source*: Author's experience).

Opportunity segments:	Isotonic sports Hydration	Wake-up stimulants	Detox Hydration	Coffee shop alternatives	100% natural drinks	Drinking more water at work	5-a-day fruit and veg
Current offers:	Football sports drinks	Red Bull	Bottled water	Own label water	Fruit juice Water	Standard coolers	Fruit juice
Growth:	Medium	High	High	High	High	High	Medium
Core target:	Sports nuts Wannabe sports nuts	Clubbers	Women on detox	Urban busy-bodies	Health conscious CSD rejectors	Enlightened workers	Families Health conscious
Volume/ Value:	Large	Medium	Medium	Large	Large	Large	Large
Relevant trends:	Growth of non-football sports	Computer gaming	Obesity/ dieting explosion	'3rd space'on every corner	Backlash against CSDs	Men getting into well-being	Government campaign on 5-a-day
	↓	↓	↓	↓	↓	↓	↓
Innovation Briefs:	Winter sports drink	All night computer gaming drink	Water for dieting	Premium 'sit and chat' soft drink	100% No additives fruit concoction	Water cooler with attitude	Fruit and veg drink

Some of the innovations in Table 6.3 have been identified and launched. No, they are not all niches.

- *Innocent/PJ/Odwalla Smoothies* are taking the soft drinks market by storm in Europe and the USA, by brining personality and panache into the dull worthy world of fruit juices.
- *Water cooler companies* are being snapped up by major players who see them as a key volume opportunity with access to the workplace.
- *Knorr Vie* Fruit and veg shots have been some of Unilever's most successful launches to date, tapping directly into the strong need for health and well-being by making 5-a-day easier.
- *Countless energy drinks* have been launched at Red Bull loving clubbers. Why has no one seen the enormous high growth area of computer gaming as the next target?

By mapping the future of the segments – building in trends analysis – we have created a far more insightful and helpful set of innovation briefs.

Write a good innovation brief

The Good, the Bad and the Bleedin' Obvious

So what should an innovation brief look like? Too many times innovation briefs are stuffed with extraneous material culled from other briefs. They extol the virtues of the existing brand while being entirely vague about the task, except in such details as the date of the next meeting, the format of the final report and the pantone reference of the core brand colour. These are bad briefs, or BOIB's, as shown in Box 6.2.

A good brief sheds light on the task in hand. It need not be long but it must be clear. The other important aspect is that the brief should fit the task. There is no law that states that each brief should be identical. Corporate machines love regularity, innovation is, by definition, trying to step beyond the regular and create the irregular. If each brief a team receives for a new innovation looks identical to the previous one, what is their take-out? Is it that innovation is a standardized business process that should be dealt with in the same manner as an expenses claim? Change each brief to transmit the essentials of the task in hand – focus the team on the challenge and leave everything else out.

What's in a good brief?

There are of course many things you could put into your brief but *less is more*. Here are my suggestions for the key headings to use. Use as small a *subset* of the following as you can to get the task across

---

Box 6.2: B.O.I.B – Bleedin' Obvious Innovation Brief

Company:	Parity Products Inc.
Brand:	MeToo™
Context:	Metoo™ is an exciting brand in the mid-quality, mid-price sector. Growth has been stable and consistent with the category in that it has been flat for two years. Premium brands are demonstrating growth can be achieved through innovation, so we want to join in.
Brand objective:	Growth (in sales and volume)
Task:	An innovation
Target:	Consumers who shop the category
Competition:	Other brands. And own label
Timing:	Next year

- *Clear vision*: Encapsulate the brief in *one sentence*. This is the CEO 'elevator pitch' if they were to ask you what your latest innovation project is. Be concise.
- *Business objective*: What are you trying to achieve? Usually in terms of target occasions or consumer groups, or financials. Whatever is the clearest measure of success for the team to shoot at.
- *Role in brand:*
  - *Brand idea* – State clearly the brand idea that should drive the innovation.
  - *Architecture fit* – Show where the new innovation will sit in the brand architecture. If this is unclear then at least indicate the preferred position and the no-go areas.
  - *Brand value drivers* – What are the key product truths to build from? What made your brand what it is today? (That it truly owns).
- *Target*: State the consumer groups you are targeting, showing how they are different from that of the core, or for which different occasions or needs you are wishing to target the same people as your core. Be specific. Add any single insight that brings them to life.
- *Source of gains*: What will people stop spending money on in order to buy this new innovation? Only use this criterion if you have a clear idea of the particular substitution.
- *Channel*: Where will this innovation be sold – *only* mention this if it is different from core.
- *'Drop-Dead' lines*: These are your key 'drop-dead' dates, important presentations, concept test timings and/or in market launch expectations.
- *Previous work*: It is critical to point the team in the direction of previous projects to plunder. The 3-Bucket principle demands that you fill Bucket 1 with any relevant existing ideas.
- *Senior experts*: Who in the senior team has some real expertise that would prove useful in building this innovation? List the stakeholders and potential contributors to enable the team to make best use of the expert's talents.

 Three-minute workout

Have a quick go in Box 6.3. Jot down in the next three minutes the essentials for your current or next innovation project. As an example, see the brief for the Calippo Innovation in Box 6.4.

Paint your vision loud and proud

Once you have defined your innovation vision don't hide it in a drawer. Or worse still, just email it out to the team. Just like a brand vision, a clear definition of the innovation

---

Box 6.3: Quick Innovation Brief

Innovation Vision: _____

**Business
Objective:** _____

Brand Idea: _____

Target: _____

Source of Gains: _____

'Drop-Dead' lines: _____

Senior Experts: _____

Box 6.4: Calippo Shots Innovation Brief. (*Source*: Author's own)

Vision:	To get teens to buy Calippo
Business Objectives:	To gain share of teen refreshment occasions, stealing from soft drinks to generate incremental revenue across the top 10 markets
Brand idea:	Freestyle Refreshment
Target:	Teens – from 12 when they stop eating water ice to 18 when they get into alcohol for refreshment
Source of gains:	Soft drinks, **not** ice cream
'Drop-dead' line:	Present to innovation board on 24th June Test market in Q1 next year
Senior experts:	Head of Ice RÖ Spanish development team – they're very keen

---

task needs to be communicated properly to the team to ensure that they have 'got it'. As innovation projects tend to be shorter than brand lifecycles (they certainly should be!) you can afford to be a little more direct and 'in your face' with your communication. Be loud and proud. Write it on a wall in big letters. Hand out T-shirts with it emblazoned on the chest. There are good reasons for 'going loud' and being outspoken about your innovation vision:

- *Forces you to commit to it*: When you go public you have to follow through.
- *Leaves people in no doubt*: When you literally paint it on the wall there is no arguing about it or room for the team to wonder if you are serious about the innovation.
- *Makes you think twice*: Is it really as crystal clear as it could be? If it is going to be up for all passing dignitaries to see then it had better be good.
- *No backing down*: Determination and influencing persistence are hallmarks of great innovators. By being so open you are making it much more difficult to change your mind or worse, dither.

- *Makes you revisit it regularly*: Having your intentions so clearly signposted helps the team to revisit the vision at each critical juncture, and to realign themselves and their ideas.

> ### VISION WARNING:
> ### YOU MIGHT GO BLAND

One trap that it is easy to fall into is to try so hard to get a snappy one-line innovation vision that you go bland. Vision blandness is a condition that blights many a marketing team. Don't be lured by its easy virtues.

Apple: Steve Jobs and the art of vision painting

When Steve Jobs retook his role as CEO of Apple he famously slashed their innovation projects from hundreds to just three: iMac, iBook and the G4 (the iPod came later). This single act of innovation clarity probably accounted for half of the turnaround in itself. He did it swiftly, clearly and publicly. No one was in any doubt as to what the priorities were. And because there were only three (Figure 6.4), everyone also knew that the boss would be all over them, so they had better make progress daily.

There were many other things that changed at Apple on Steve Jobs' return, but in my view, that one decision put Apple back on top. They had the focus and clarity to make their considerable innovation talents pay. Talents that were mired in a long list of worthy, well thought through but unfocused projects.

This was not a one-off – a lucky dip on his first day in charge. Steve Jobs excels at visioning. He is continually stating what he *will* do. Most CEOs, when they stand up in front of the world's press and financial markets, are talking about what they have *done*. Whether it's last year's results, a successful new launch or a merger or acquisition, it's always in the past tense. Steve Jobs is stuck in the future tense. He nods to past success in a way that suggests 'that's only the beginning' and has his eyes, mind and heart locked on his *next* move.

He commits himself, and his entire staff and resources publicly at MacWorld. When he delivers his keynote speech he talks about what will ship in the next few weeks and what will be achieved by the next MacWorld. The ostensible audience is the tech world at large – his competitors, loyal fans and the financial markets. But I believe the true target for much of his speech is his own people. He is visioning. He's doing it very big and loud and publicly so that even the cleaners at their Cupertino HQ know what the priorities are for the next year.

Macintosh

The story of the development and launch of the Apple Macintosh reads like a Hollywood movie, with setbacks and surprises and daring programmers solving seemingly impossible

iMac

iBook   Mac G4

Figure 6.4: iMac, iBook, and G4 – Apple's turnaround products.

problems in the nick of time. The driving force behind it was Steve Jobs the visionary. His ability to inspire his team on and on to surmount impossible hurdles and go beyond (way beyond) accepted norms is a lesson in innovation visioning.

Steve Jobs didn't start the Macintosh project, it was an unofficial team led by Jeff Raskin who started the ball rolling. Steve took over when he was looking for something new to pour his energy into and the little renegade bunch working on their idea of a small, low-cost machine caught his imagination.

His first act was to hire a team of evangelists who shared his passion for hardware. The computer, already named Macintosh after Jeff Raskin's favourite apple (the McIntosh), was just a jumble of parts. It truly came to life when one of Steve's new employees, in one marathon 24-hour session, got the first images up on the screen.

This is when Steve Jobs, the innovation visionary, set the goal that galvanized the team and ignited the project. He announced to the team that this bundle of circuit board and wires would be on sale to the public in 12 months. It was an impossible timeline, but Jobs wouldn't budge. The vision was set, and the team 'drank his Kool Aid'!

Having set such a challenging vision he was prepared to pull rank on anyone and anything in the business to get the team what they wanted. He showed that he was as committed to the vision as he expected his team to be.

By expressing the vision as a launch date he created a highly visual, tangible end point; everyone knew what that meant for their area – graphics, disk drives, software, etc.

He reinforced the vision and energized his team at each visit. He didn't set up meetings, he would just drop into someone's cubicle, ask what he or she was working on, and suggest immediate improvements – to make it smaller, faster, cooler looking. Quite quickly the team knew that they had to have something cool and new to show him when he visited unannounced. His vision was being turned into action by the hour.

In one famous incident when the team were working late, eating the pizzas that Jobs always ordered, he came in holding a telephone book. He slammed it on the table and said: "I want it be no bigger than this – all PC's are too bulky." He left before anyone could contest his command or offer him pizza. Again it was a seemingly impossible goal, brilliantly

Figure 6.5: The Apple Macintosh '1984' launch advert.

and simply visualized – a telephone book – it galvanized the team to break the rules and find ways to fit an entire computer into a smaller, neater package.

To reinforce the vision publicly six months later, he bet rival project, the Lisa, $5000 that his Macintosh would ship before theirs, even though their project had been running officially for two years. The fact that you've never heard of the Apple Lisa says it all!

Eventually the Macintosh project became official. The board moved the launch date back into 1983. Macintosh launched at the super bowl with their legendary 1984 advert directed by Ridley Scott of Aliens fame (see Figure 6.5). The accessibly priced $1300 graphically based computer was an instant hit. Steve Jobs' vision had become a reality.

Apple summary

- Make your vision tangible
- Keep reinforcing the vision
- Demonstrate your personal commitment to the vision
- Order pizza

Key takeouts

1 No cookie-cutter processes. The design of your innovation process needs to be built around where you are trying to get to.
2 The clearer and more tangible the end result is envisioned, the more efficient and successful your innovation project will be.
3 Don't let delays slip in and kill your project from within. Create big public deadlines that galvanise everyone.
4 Great footballers move to where the ball *will* be. Envisage the way the market *will* be to better target your new ideas.
5 The clearer, tighter and more focused a brief you can write, the easier the innovation task becomes.

Checklist : Destination

	Yes	*No*
Does everyone have the same clear simple brief in mind?	☐	☐
Is your innovation goal truly in line with your brand vision?	☐	☐

- Is your innovation vision truly differentiated? Could your competitors not be working to the same brief?
- Is your process tailored to overcome the challenges, not just tailored to fit the constraints?
- Is your vision for the innovation proudly on display for all to see?
- Do your inputs allow you to map out the future of the category, not just the present?

 Handover

Now that you have defined and brought to life a clear vision for the innovation, you need some good ideas. The next chapter is all about how to get them. Lots of them.

Rocketing: Combustion

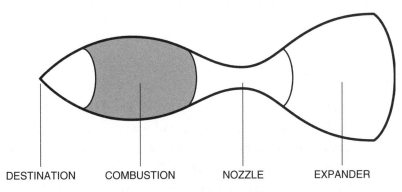

CHAPTER 7

DESTINATION   COMBUSTION   NOZZLE   EXPANDER

The Innovation Rocket

 ## Headlines

Combustion is at the heart of the Rocketing approach – how to create ideas. It tackles the key issue in current innovation processes of not having enough high-quality ideas. There are three parts to good Combustion: creating a continuous source of potent insight 'fuel', running multiple ideas ignition sessions in parallel and managing ideas effectively to get the most from them using the 3-Bucket principle.

Not enough good ideas

The key issue with innovation projects is not having enough good-quality ideas. Anyone can produce 50 ideas that are random or wacky – and may well prove to be good fodder – but it's very hard to guarantee to come up with 50 good ideas. Because ideas feel easy to acquire, not much time is allocated to ideation – one day at the start of a project is not uncommon. Having lots of low-quality initial ideas gives the impression of having plenty to work with. But this is false.

Ideas don't grow on trees

In the idealized, fairytale world of innovation where funnels produce perfect new products to launch each time, ideas are supposed to just appear at the start of the process. This is treated as the 'easy' bit of innovation – just come up with some ideas, go on, it's simple!

We all instinctively know that great ideas at the start are more likely to produce great product launches at the end, but how can you be sure you get a good quantity of good-quality ideas into your projects?

A different approach to ideation

Once your vision is set and the brief is clear, it is time to set off the combustion process. But rather than sliding straight into a one-day brainstorming session with the same old team, it's time to plan out and embark on a workplan that involves a much wider team, different styles and inputs and guarantees a higher quantity and quality of ideas. This is not some weird new Eastern philosophy that means you have to start sitting cross-legged on the floor chanting to the Gods of ideas and writing everything in purple. This is just smarter brainstorming. It is about creating a continuous source of potent insight fuel, with the right mix of techniques to ignite this fuel and convert it most efficiently into ideas. Then you need new ways to harness the stream of ideas to enable you to get the most out of them towards your goal.

The following sections outline the method:

7.1 *Continuous Insight Fuel* – non-stop sources of potent insight fuel
7.2 *Multiple Ignition in parallel* – multiple processes to ignite insight into ideas
7.3 *3 Bucket Principle* – effective ideas management

7.1   CONTINUOUS INSIGHT FUEL

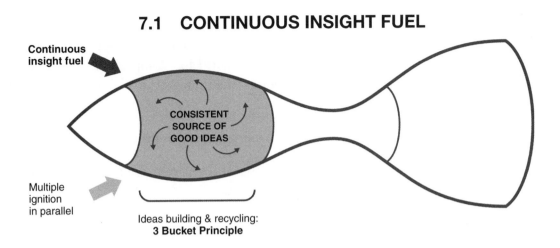

Continuous insight fuel

CONSISTENT SOURCE OF GOOD IDEAS

Multiple ignition in parallel

Ideas building & recycling:
3 Bucket Principle

From insight to fuel

Insight is most often characterized as answers to questions. For innovation this is not a helpful thought. Insight managers need to rethink their role as fuel suppliers. When this is the starting point then it is clear that the search must be for the most potent mix of insight fuel.

True insights are as rare as unicorns, and marketers are all after true insights. But these are hard to find and need a lot of work to acquire. Formal primary research (qualitative and quantitative) is the most obvious tool for bringing true insights into an innovation process, but it is by no means the only one, and it won't be dealt with in detail in this book. The important thing to bear in mind is how to get maximum value from all the research that is done. Millions of dollars are spent each year by corporations on research and much of the value is never extracted because it is secondary, i.e. it is not the bald data alone that holds all the value, but how it can inspire thinking among the team. Too often marketers assume that insight means market research – what they *hear* in focus groups or the *data* that emerges from quantitative studies. This is a mistake.

Marketing Mistake :	Insight = Consumer Research

It doesn't help that most research departments are now called Consumer Insight Centres, even when 90% of their time is spent briefing and managing consumer research. Young marketers can't really be blamed for the confusion!

Aha!

An insight is an 'Aha!' moment, something that leads to action. If new information does not lead directly to action, then it is a finding not an insight. Most companies are awash with findings. True insights are usually rough diamonds hiding in a heap of findings and need careful polishing before they shine.

> **Insight** = A deep new understanding that leads to action

There are many other definitions of true insights, but this one has been the most useful for defining innovation insights.

360° Insight

By sourcing insights from all sorts of different places, with a wide range of techniques and covering off all parts of the marketing mix, you create the most potent insight fuel. Commonly called 360° insight, it encourages you to source insight from all angles. One way to drive this process into your innovation projects is to create a 360° insight source list at the start (see Figure 7.1).

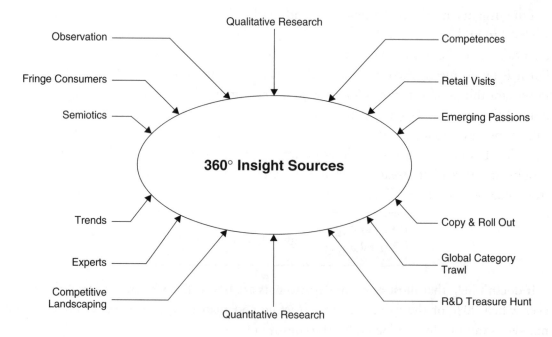

Figure 7.1: 360° Insight Sources.

Use the list to kick off multiple investigations; they don't all have to be big, agency-led studies. Asking your secretaries/assistants to go out and experience a new product and report back may yield great insights as well as involve them in interesting work. Ask teams from other markets to take on specific responsibilities – it doesn't always have to be done by your team.

360° Insight Sources

Qualitative research: How to get more insight from Qual

At face value, qualitative research should explain *why* people do certain things. A great way to get more insight from the work you already do is to ask your qualitative agency to present their findings more visually and interactively. For instance, you could role play how you wanted consumers to react when you confront them with the concept, then compare and contrast this with what they actually did. Asking your agency to script the probable responses forces everyone to think about real people and closes the 'us and them' gap between marketers and consumers. It's too easy to take on face value phrases like 'Consumers didn't want the brand to stretch that far'. Ordinary people don't think about stretch and brands that way – spend more time interrogating *why* they reacted as they did to your idea, and leave the brand strategy for the summary discussion. You'll get more powerful insights that way.

When the Australian car breakdown service NRMA developed a new consumer segmentation, the results were presented as full size picture cut-outs of each typology. The team walked around and 'met' each one, then got to know them and started creating ideal services for each. They were expecting two hours of PowerPoint and strong coffee. What they got was more stimulating, insightful, memorable and productive.

Quantitative research: How to get more insight from Quant

Quantitative research should define how many, when and who exactly does *what*. Too often quant debriefs just end up being a flood of data – endless charts of this variable against the other making it very easy to lose the focus of the research. Good quant presentations are, in fact, very short. Challenge your quant agency to deliver the insight, backed by data, not just the data backed by more data.

Challenge your quant agency to:

- Present the insights in just *one chart*.
- Write the *story* behind the data.
- Spend one-third of the debrief presenting charts and two-thirds generating insights as a team.

When Unilever ice cream received the debrief for their 14-country global segmentation they didn't get very much. In fact, they had given a very clear brief to the research agency: we want *one* chart. This chart focused the agency right down to the nub of the issue and made for a short presentation (30 minutes) followed by a much more interactive and useful session where the reams of data were used to answer each specific question. The result is that because of its simplicity the segmentation was adopted globally in a very short time, creating real value for all.

Observation: Watch don't just listen

Turn off your intellectual/verbal filter and just *watch* what people do. It is often very different to what they *say* they do. When sitting in a focus group consumers are 'performing' – exposing their habits in front of their peers. There are bound to be things they forget or just leave out. Watching people uncovers a whole new world of insight. Go to where consumers consume/use your product and just watch: in a bar, at their homes, out and about. Go to your primary channel and watch how they choose products in your category, and compare it to how they shop for others.

A vintage problem

When Southcorp, then Australia's biggest wine exporter, were rethinking their brand portfolio with Added Value, my suggestion was to watch consumers choosing their wine in store. The prevailing thinking at the time was that consumers spent quality time considering different options before making their final choice. 'That's what people say in focus groups' was the confident claim, 'and our quant data says they spend four times as long in front of wine fixture as any other in a supermarket.' When they actually *observed* people in front of the wine shelf, the truth became abundantly clear – people were bewildered. The time they spent was in confusion not consideration, ending up most likely with a choice based on 'I'll just take this one – I hope it's OK'. The team immediately saw that more brands = more confusion (not more choice) and set about consolidating their offer into three flagship brands: Penfolds, Rosemount and Lindemans.

Fringe consumers: talk to the wrong people

When exploring new pack designs or communications then it's essential to talk to your core consumers. But when you are looking for new ideas, ways to resegment your market and create new categories, then it's time to talk to people who don't fit your target. These are people who may use your product very occasionally or in a different way. They may come from a radically different social group than your core users. Talk to them, the results will be surprising.

Red light insight

When Kimberly Klarke wanted to create growth for their Kotex sanitary protection brand in Latin America they needed some fresh insight on menstruation. They already had mountains of research among the same core users as their competitors; they knew all the core needs, occasions and associated benefits of good protection. They needed a new angle on it.

They talked to prostitutes.

For this fringe group, feminine hygiene is clearly a big issue and their needs, techniques and relationships with sanitary protection brands were different to regular consumers. A totally fresh insight was born: menstruation is a sign of health and wellness, affirmation of true womanhood and a respite from everyday 'duties' – a time for recuperation and pampering. This led to innovation around the benefit of 'time for me' rather than 'liberation' where all the other brands were focused.

Semiotics: cultural body language

Most markets have heard of or have had some experience of 'semiotics' but it is still not well understood. The best explanation is that it reveals the unspoken codes or body language of brands, categories or cultures. As it is done by experts and academics and not with consumers, it isn't research. It is a very powerful tool when used correctly and utter nonsense when misused. If it isn't introduced properly to audiences, or if the brief is too broad, then the result is a very interesting, sometimes shocking but always confusing presentation that leaves people bewildered. When used correctly it can cut right to the nub of complex multi-market issues and unleash brand revolutionizing ideas instantly.

Off milk

Tetrapak wanted to capture some of the growth and volume of fresh milk in the UK. They wanted to try and improve the freshness credentials of their UHT Longlife milk. Unfortunately, green cows and white graphics were nothing in combat with the unspoken codes of the category that were decoded by the semioticians.

Semiotic analysis of UHT milk packaging codes

Code 1: 'Longlife' → never **ever** goes off → not living
Code 2: Square, hermetically sealed box → coffin

Thus the conclusion was that there was an unspoken communication from their product: UHT milk packaging signified death. Tetrapak then spent no more time and effort trying to convince people that UHT was fresh. Instead they designed the Tetra-top pack to house genuine fresh milk for the dairies.

Trends: sense cultural shifts

We've all been there – the trends presentation; someone from insight presents 46 PowerPoint slides on demographics and 'single person households are on the increase' stuff. Everyone says 'how interesting' and leaves. Trends don't have to be like this!

Good trends engender action. They set off fireworks in people's heads. The most important part of a trends presentation is that they should be *inspiring*.

It is important to get fresh trends every time you need them, as showing the same charts again and again will illicit the same responses, and trends, by definition, should evolve.

- Boards (Figure 7.2) are an excellent way to bring trends to life for use in workshops. They can be introduced in overview and then people can work with each one to generate ideas. It also means they stay up as inspiration all through the session.

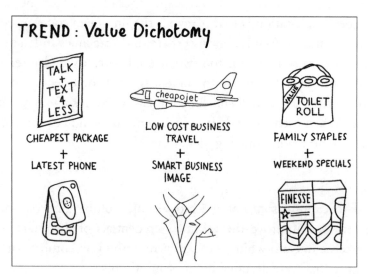

Figure 7.2: A trend board.

Figure 7.3: A headline from the future.

- Creating 'Headlines from the future' (Figure 7.3) are another way to turn dull data and charts into inspiring inputs. Extrapolate a trend to a ridiculous extent, then imagine the sensationalist headlines that might ensue. Headlines like this ensued in a brainstorming with Levis. They inspired the joint exploration with Phillips of electronics implanted into clothes – phones, MP3 players, radios etc – and innovations are beginning to emerge.

Experts: meet smart people

An often overlooked and very potent source of insight and fresh perspective is to talk to people who have particular expertise or knowledge of the category or consumers you are targeting.

Chocs away!

A major chocolate business wanted to find new paths to growth and a route through the diet and health wave that is engulfing the western world. They gathered two groups of experts in two key countries to have a discussion on the issue of obesity and confectionery.

They cast the net deliberately wide, looking for different sorts and sources of expertise to create a lively debate. They found:

- Dietician/nutritionist
- Fashion editor for *Elle* magazine

- Cosmetic surgeon
- Government food scientist
- Doctor (GP)
- Weight Watchers organizer
- Personal trainer
- Lady who owns a clothes shop for larger women

The experts sat in a circle with a moderator; the marketing team sat around the outside of the room to listen. It was held at a smart apartment, not a grubby viewing facility. The video capture was not a wall-mounted 'seeing eye' but a professional videographer.

The session itself was very lively indeed – particular highlights were watching the Dietician and Weight Watchers organizer challenge the fashion editor on her use of stick thin models. (Her robust reply – 'normal' sized models don't sell magazines, we tried it.) Also, the woman with the dress shop for larger ladies admitting that she always carried a chocolate bar in her handbag 'for emergencies', and watching the medical experts being appalled at how chocolate was more trusted than the medical profession for sorting out highs and lows.

The insights that emerged inspired the team to refine their existing ideas and were then expanded and explored in other insight sessions with consumers.

Experts' summary

- Get a diverse group of experts
- Treat them with respect
- Attend the session yourself

Competitive landscaping: see what's out there

It is too easy to assume that you know your own market. In some corner of a foreign shelf there may be a new entrant you don't know about. Competitive landscaping is the process for trawling your market and key adjacent markets for any and all offers. Draw up a list of all categories adjacent to your own. Divide them between your team and ask them to go out to several stores and buy examples of each. Gather them together on a table and have a good rummage about for ideas on any part of the mix.

This is especially powerful for global teams as it educates everyone about each other's markets in a very tangible way, as well as providing tremendous insight into what the consumers are faced with when making their choices.

Teenage ice cream

This process was most illuminating for the team tasked with growing Calippo. I have detailed the case study for Calippo Shots earlier in this book, but the very excellent brief for this innovation came from rethinking the competitive landscape (Figure 7.4). In the ice cream team's day-to-day work they were thinking through a model that defined the ice cream world. Once they thought through the competitive landscape from a teenager's point of view, the map looked very different:

For teenagers water-ice was competing as a snack, not an ice cream. That meant that its closest category competitors were the seemingly distant soft drinks, mints and confectionery. The team then changed the innovation brief to attack and steal share from Carbonated Soft Drinks. This is how Calippo Shots was developed.

R&D treasure hunt: get with the tech

A huge amount of time in innovation projects is spent arguing over the likely feasibility of one idea over the next. And most often it occurs between people who are ill equipped

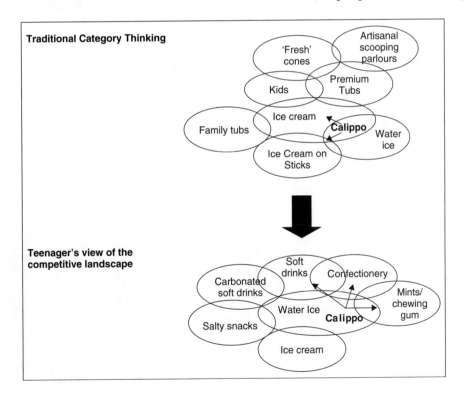

Figure 7.4: Water Ice competitive landscapes.

to judge. Giving time at an early stage for the R&D team to 'strut their stuff' can open everyone's eyes to just what could be possible. The key here is to do a Treasure Hunt, have fun, get carried away with the whole Willy Wonka technology of it all, and you will be amazed what the techies can do when you show interest and give them centre stage. The key to any technical presentation is an insistence on simple, non-technical, idiot-proof explanations. No formulae, molecular diagrams or tech-speak definitions. Focus them on telling you (in layman's terms) what it *is*, and what it *does* for consumers. Above all – get prototypes made.

In my time I have come across the following amazing technologies in sessions such as these:

- Transparent milk
- No-poo dog food
- Belly button laxatives

Is this Frankenstein science destined for the trash or tomorrow's blockbuster products? Who knows. Figure 7.5 shows a simple structured pro-forma I use when briefing R&D to present their ideas.

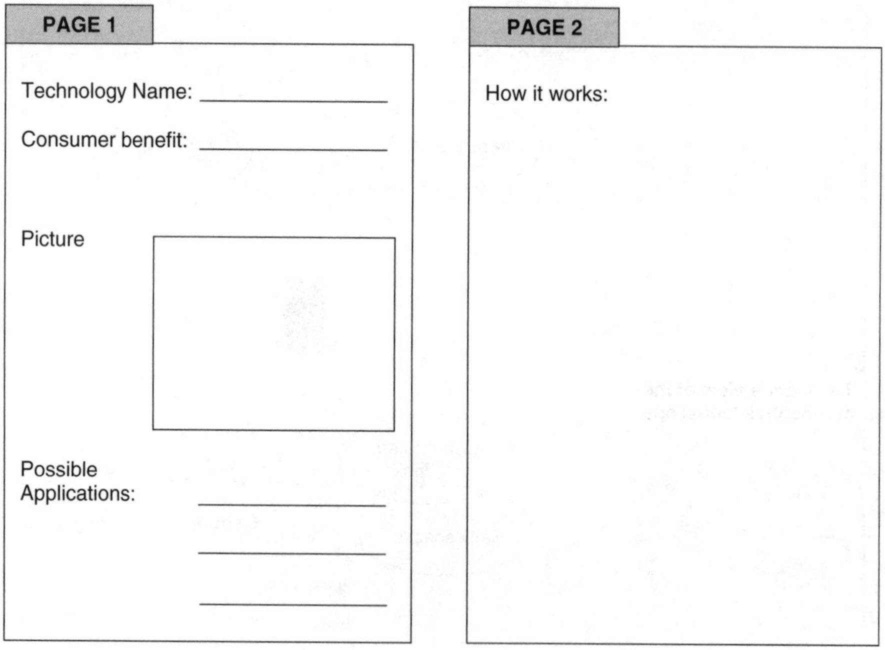

PAGE 1	PAGE 2
Technology Name: _____ Consumer benefit: _____ Picture Possible Applications: _____ _____ _____	How it works:

Figure 7.5: R&D treasure hunt briefing proforma.

Global Category Trawl : The Weird and Wonderful

It is constantly fascinating to see what is going on in the rest of the world. Different cultures, consumer needs and market structures create totally different opportunities and offers all the time. Unlike competitive landscaping, which is focused on specific products in specific adjacent categories, this is about seeking out the quirky emergent stuff that's not mainstream yet.

Pick emergent markets or strongly different ones like Japan (different to almost everywhere!) and brief an agency or talented individual to go digging. What is hidden in a few oddball shops in London may have a huge cult following in San Francisco. What has been around for ages in Mexico may be the next big thing in mainland Europe.

When looking for new and interesting food ideas for a German business in 2003 the team found an obscure drink in a quirky London health shop – an Aloe Vera drink. When the team had a young trend scout look around Japan's shops and markets they found a whole host of Aloe Vera food products: drinks, yoghurts and snacks. Today Aloe Vera drinks and foods (Figure 7.6) are now emerging in the UK and Germany in health food outlets. How long will it be before they become mainstream?

Copy and roll out: go ahead – cheat

Why does every new product idea need to be 100% original? Even when we think it is, there's always some brand somewhere in the world that did it first. So why not go with the flow and cheat?

Figure 7.6: Aloe Vera – an emergent food.

Figure 7.7: Magnum Double.

Looking at what is successful in other markets then copying it and rolling it out better and faster than the originator is a fantastic way to secure growth quickly.

Magnum force

When the team responsible for Magnum ice cream got a call from their sales manager in New Zealand they were taken aback; Nestlé had innovated the 'large ice cream covered in good chocolate on a curvy stick' formula and created the Mississippi Mud Pie – an ice cream with two layers of chocolate and chocolate fondant in between. They took it straight to their development colleagues and in no time created the Magnum Double (Figure 7.7) – two layers of chocolate sandwiching a caramel fondant. They then rolled it out globally faster than Nestlé did. The result was a resounding success and growth building for Magnum.

Emerging passions: be cool

What's new in culture that is catching on? There's so much happening around the world that there is no way you can stay abreast of all of it, but there may be real value in getting a better understanding of new passion areas that are growing fast.

In 2006 there are some emerging passions that marketers in almost all categories should be aware of. Are you?

As of 2007, are you in the know on:

- *Computer Gaming* – bigger than the film or music industries
- *My Space* – the peer-to-per networking site that is redefining the entertainment industry's value chain
- *Women's Golf* – fashion, TV, publishing and footwear should take note
- *Podcasting* – a global medium, channel and cultural influencer

---

Get yourself and your team immersed. A short sharp session with some experts doing a show and tell, followed by an hour's brainstorming for opportunities across the whole mix will do wonders for those seeking inspiration.

Retail visits: go shopping

Every time you have a meeting abroad – go shopping. Have a nose around various stores and take your little black book. It is amazing what you can find and the opportunities and ideas that can emerge.

The power of the retailer is on the increase, so time spent thinking like one is valuable for your whole team. Look at:

- product siting
- new private label offers
- point of sale
- promotions
- packaging
- shopper behaviour

Don't just visit your own shelf, have a look at anything that catches your eye as new, different or clever.

A digestive diversion

The global brand team for an over-the-counter digestive health medicine took an hour off to go shopping in the middle of a two-day brand stretch workshop. They had got into a cul-de-sac around new active ingredients and registration issues, so were glad of a little diversion.

Instead of poring over the healthcare aisle in the supermarket, they looked at confectionery. Here in front of them was a totally new way to segment their offer – by occasion. Chocolate was being successfully marketed to different occasions just by changing the size and shape. Surely the same occasion-based thinking could apply to digestive health remedies? Day 2 was a very productive session!

Competences: work the canteen

"*If only we knew what we knew*" is a cry that goes up many times in major multinationals. All sorts of expertise and competence exist in businesses that could be applied successfully outside their primary area if only people in the right places knew about it.

Figure 7.8: An internal cross-fertilisation innovation mechanism.

Make a list of all the people you know in interesting parts of your business – especially other operating units. Get your boss and your team to do the same. Call them, email them and invite them for a coffee in the canteen (Figure 7.8). Explain your vision and your issues. Then listen.

Summary

A useful tool to have is an insight checklist (see Table 7.1). Stick it to the wall or tack it to the back of an innovation brief as a handy reminder. Use it to inspire your teams to look wider for ideas and insight during every innovation project. Don't assume that it means that more time and money needs to be spent; it's intended to expand your *thinking*, not your *budget*.

Table 7.1: 360° insight checklist.

Insight Source	Description	Timing	Resp.	$
Observation	• Go to where consumers consume/use your product and just watch			
Fringe consumers	• Interview people you've never talked to before, at the (scary) fringes			
Semiotics	• Look at the body language of your brand and category. Use expert Semioticians			
Trends	• Look at what is changing in culture and society. Get fresh trends each year			
Experts	• Talk to experts in your category; media pundits, consultants, academics, etc.			
Competitive landscaping	• Gather competitive products from all adjacent categories and rethink your market.			
R&D treasure hunt	• Get R&D to show you what they've got in their cupboard early on. It's surprising			
Global Category Trawl	• Look for weird and wonderful stuff from emergent markets like Japan. Go broad			
Copy & roll out	• Look at what is successful in other markets in your category. Copy it			
Emerging passions	• Get in the know on what is cool and emergent. Ask yourself why . . .			
Retail Visits	• Put yourself in the shoes of the retailer • Go to a store and experience the buying 'moment of truth'			
Competences	• What are your company's competences? • Look across other business units			
Qualitative research	• Make the feedback visual and interactive			
Quantitative research	• Focus on the insight not just the data			

7.2 MULTIPLE IGNITION IN PARALLEL

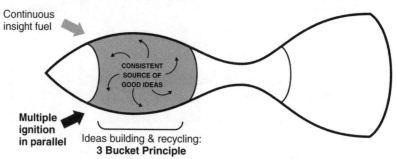

Igniting the insight fuel

You have defined a clear destination for your innovation. You've designed the innovation process to suit the needs of your particular challenge. You've organized for insights to be gathered from far and wide, new and old sources. You've even done some primary observation yourself, interviewed fringe consumers way off your normal target and immersed yourself and your team into some bizarre new consumer passion areas. All you need now is to turn it all into good ideas. This is the crux of the Rocketing process – igniting the 360° insight fuel into an explosion of high-quality ideas. The new paradigm for ideation that can deliver more ideas at higher quality is to do multiple brainstorming sessions simultaneously.

Parallel processing

Are you into computer architecture? Do you know Moore's Law – that computer processing power will double every 24 months? Gordon E. Moore was the co-founder of Intel who led the charge in making his own law come true (Figure 7.9). The kick-off point for this explosion in computing power was the invention of parallel processing by Californian Danny Hillis when he was just an undergraduate. The basic concept is easy, but the ramifications are immense.

Computer processor manufacturers were looking at a long slow haul to double the processing power of their early chips until the simple idea of parallel processing dropped into their laps. Suddenly they were dealing with an exponential growth curve – just by splitting the tasks between two processors alongside each other. The resulting increase in computations per second was more than double, it was to the power of 2/3/4... according to the number of processors the tasks were divided among. Put those processors onto one

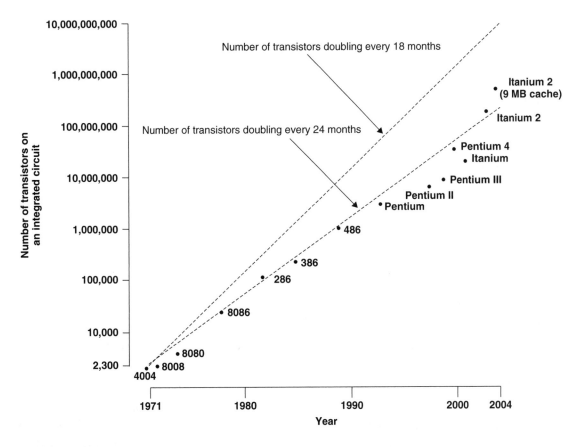

Figure 7.9: Moore's Law – processing power doubles every 24 months.

chip and bingo! You have a microprocessor – the fundamental building block of today's computer-enhanced world.

Applying parallel processing to innovation

By splitting the ideation into multiple separate parallel steps it hugely increases the quantity **and** quality of the ideas that are delivered. If we follow the principle of Moore's Law further, it means that the power of your ideas should increase exponentially as you parallel process. Now that would be worth having!

How it works

In a standard innovation process the brainstorming or ideation is plotted in as a step in the linear process – just as in our fictitious process example. (Figure 7.10)

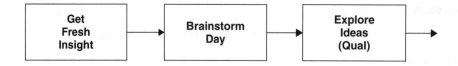

Figure 7.10: A standard ideation process.

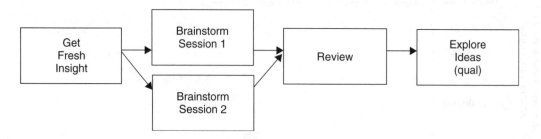

Figure 7.11: A parallel brainstorming process.

This session will undoubtedly be held in a stimulating location, have a facilitator and include several people with a 'creative' mindset. This is all good stuff. Now consider a parallel brainstorming process as in Figure 7.11.

The simple addition of a **second** brainstorming session that happens **simultaneously** with the first and uses exactly the **same inputs**, brings huge advantages: it can be held in totally different circumstances – a different country perhaps – and use a different type of participant. With the addition of a simple review step, the breadth of ideas and thus opportunity to stretch thinking to new areas is increased by a factor of 2. Consider the ways in which this second parallel session could be run to bring in new thinking to your project:

- in a second country/language/culture
- entirely with creatives
- with people who do **not** know your brand
- with teenagers

... and the possibilities continue. With modest extra resources you can bring tremendous richness into your project with just one extra parallel session.

My recommendation is that this is the minimum you do. The optimum route is to run several parallel sessions to maximize your idea power. In our fictitious example process, a better number of sessions might have been four (see Figure 7.12)

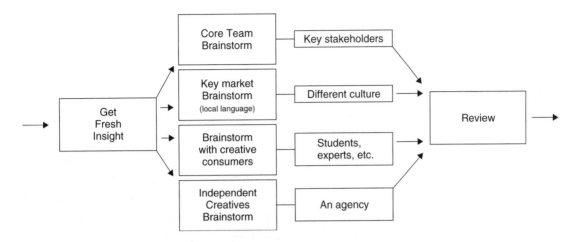

Figure 7.12: A fourly way parallel ideation process.

You must be careful to balance practicality with the desire for breadth, but the extra resource needed at this stage in an innovation process is relatively minor compared to the benefits it brings.

> # Tip
>
> Don't ask all sessions to produce output in the same format. The diversity of styles will itself bring value to the ideas

The benefits of parallel processing are:

1 *More ideas!*
2 *More risk*: To be able to make mistakes (i.e. suggest poor ideas) is a fantastic boon to any innovation process. If you only have one session then you cannot afford to have bad ideas, thus you tend to be conservative and screen out directions that feel uncomfortable. Parallel processing allows you to have loads of terrible ideas without worrying. This is the principle benefit of parallel processing as the less fear of mistakes you have, the more unfettered your imagination and the better quality are your ideas. Every innovation process should have an ideas session that produces rubbish. Pure, unadulterated rubbish. That way you can be sure you are pushing the boundaries and having some fresh thoughts.
3 *More engagement*: This gives a terrific opportunity for key stakeholders to get really involved and feel they are contributing tangibly.

Parallel processing can obviously be taken to greater lengths of duplication, right up to running two innovation projects alongside each other against the same opportunity.

Lisa and Mac

Perhaps one of the greatest cases of parallel processing was at Apple Computer in the early days before Macintosh, when the Apple II was their lead product. In 1979 a project was instigated to create the next generation of Apple computers that would drive success to new levels. It was named 'Lisa' by Steve Jobs after his estranged daughter (Apple employees would often play a game to guess what the letters LISA could stand for in computerese). The project had a staff of 24 engineers, separate premises and a large budget signed off by the board. They visited the Xerox Parc Innovation Centre and came away with inspiration for many of the key Apple innovations we know today. Over in a corner of the Apple II development labs was Jeff Raskin who had the idea to create a new Apple computer that was cheap enough to appeal to a real mass market, the Macintosh (Figure 7.13), rather than Lisa's premium price position for 'serious' computer users, Apple's existing core market in the early days of personal computers (Figure 7.14).

Steve Jobs, as mentioned in Chapter 6, championed this unofficial project in direct competition to the Lisa, inspiring his team to work all hours to achieve the impossible. Lisa, on the other hand, was run on more professional lines and proceeded resolutely to develop robust new technologies in user interface, disk storage, graphics capability and a host of other areas.

The Mac team were ready to launch first, even though theirs had been a shorter development. Lisa, after five years and many millions of dollars, was still some way off readiness. The Mac launch was done with typically unique flair by Jobs – and the rest, as they say, was history.

Figure 7.13: Apple Macintosh – a product of parallel innovation processing.

Figure 7.14: Apple Lisa – its failure was Apple's gain.

The Lisa was eventually launched at a price of $10 000. Its premium user target were not interested in this expensive machine which, in practical terms, could do no more than its sleeker, cheaper, cooler cousin. The Lisa was discontinued and duly forgotten.

Without Apple's ability to parallel process significant innovation projects, it would simply no longer be around. The Lisa's failure was a key component in Macintosh's success.

Practical Ignition Tools

There are many books and training courses on personal creativity and brainstorming, so there is no need to take creativity from first principles. Below are some practical tools and processes that anyone can use to ignite ideas within a parallel-processing workplan:

- Different types of brainstorming session
- 10 brainstorming techniques anyone can do
- Types of concepts and which to use.

Ignition tools: different types of brainstorming session

Not all brainstorming sessions are alike, nor should they be. It's important to have someone in your team, (or ideally all of you) who is trained in how to run ideas sessions. This enables

Table 7.2: Different type of brainstorming session.

Type	Objective	Techniques to try	Location and style
Focused	• To generate ideas for a specific target, need and/or occasion in a particular category with a known product type	• Role play • Heaven and hell • Random word game	• On or off site • Half to full day • High energy from the start
Blue sky	• To generate ideas across a broad spectrum of categories with any number of possible products	• Break category rules • Corporation takeover • Film star takeover	• Off-site • 1 to 3 days • Take time needed to get out of 'normal business' mode
Insight platform	• To generate ideas against a set of defined consumer insights	• Cross referencing • Role play • Consumer immersion	• Off site in a consumer space (bar, home etc.) • 1 to 2 days • Get immersed in consumer world
Quickie	• To generate ideas quickly stimulated by a specific fresh input	• Yes, and ... • Colours/music • Trend extrapolation	• On site/wherever you are • 40 mins to 2 hrs + • High energy • Small group (2–5)

NB. Any technique can be used in any session

you to easily hold quickie impromptu sessions after insightful inputs without much (or any) planning. For more planned brainstorming sessions, hire an external facilitator. This will free your whole team to focus on ideas and will push you out of your comfort zone by using new and different techniques.

The key types of session are laid out in Table 7.2 together with the techniques to try first in each.

Focused

In this session you have a very tight and well articulated brief with strong constraints, typically during a major innovation project, or to solve a specific line extension issue. Scottish Courage wanted a drink to target young women who were getting bored of Bacardi Breezers. They knew the target, the occasions, the need and the strength of the drink they wanted. The result was a funky wine cooler called Bliss (Figure 7.15).

Figure 7.15: Bliss wine based premium packaged drink.

Blue Sky

In this case you are looking for the unknown and considering big steps to take you into long-term growth. You may be wanting to rethink your entire category approach to unlock new growth.

Bertolli, Unilever's olive oil based food brand, were looking for non-FMCG sources of growth from their brand idea of 'Authentic Italian Joy for Food'. A blue sky session introduced the idea of contemporary pasta bars. This concept, titled the 'Bertolli Café' is currently on trial in Holland, should you fancy a bowl of fresh pasta!

Insight platform

In this case prior research has identified a series of significant consumer insights that you wish to explore to see what new offers might be created to address them.

Vodafone reviewed a series of insights summarized out of a year's research. One was that older consumers didn't want high technology, they just wanted to talk to people easily. The resulting innovation, Vodafone Simply (Figure 7.16), has been a huge success across multiple markets.

Quickie

When you have just heard an inspiring presentation or speech, or when something new and significant has occurred in your market – do a quickie.

Figure 7.16: Vodafone Simply – an insight driven innovation.

When Coca-Cola heard that Gatorade was to launch in Europe, they held a quick ideas session. They agreed to launch a pan-European energy drink to block Gatorade, in 90 days. The result was Powerade, as detailed in Chapter 6.

Ignition tools: 10 brainstorming techniques anyone can do

There are many techniques to create ideas in brainstorming sessions. Table 7.3 provide 10 simple techniques culled from 10 years of ideation that you can do yourself:

1   Heaven and hell

Get into the teams.

	Heaven	*Hell*
Step 1	Write the best of all possible outcomes for your brand.	Write the worst of all possible outcomes from your brand.
Step 2	Swap and force yourselves to turn each item into a practical positive idea for the brand.	

Table 7.3: 10 brainstorming techniques anyone can do.

	Technique	Description	Time to do
1.	Heaven and hell	• Write the worst of all possible innovations (Hell) • Turn each into a practical positive idea (Heaven)	30 mins
2.	Role play	• Create a picture & pen portrait of your consumer • Role play it back to the group as idea stimulus	45 mins 45 mins
3.	Random word game	• 2–4 people do random word association in turn • Rest of team listen and generate ideas	15 mins
4.	Break category rules	• List all spoken & unspoken rules of your category • Break each rule to create a new idea	30 mins 30 mins
5.	(a) Corporate takeover	• List key success factors of a big successful brand • Imagine their management team takes over	30 mins
	(b) Personality takeover	• List the key qualities of a well known personality	30 mins
6.	Cross referencing	• Populate 2 axes with key aspects of your brand • Force connections between all to find new ideas	45 mins
7.	Consumer immersion	• Go to a consumer hang out; bar, home, shop . . . • Watch, listen & learn then create ideas	60 mins
8.	Yes, and . . .	• Build on others ideas instantly by reacting with 'Yes, and (my idea)'.	5 mins
9.	Colours/Music	• Write down all associations to music or a colour • Use associations to create new ideas	15 mins
10.	Trends extrapolation	• Take a trend and image it dominates culture • Turn implications into ideas for your brand	30 mins

2 Role play

Really getting yourself into the consumer's lives by role-playing them, or specific occasions or needs

Step 1 Create a picture of two or more your target consumers using images torn out of magazines and list key needs and occasions.

Step 2 Present your consumer by role playing them: introduce yourself by name, explain where you live and what a typical day is like. Other team members listen and capture ideas then ask questions of the 'consumer' about new insights, product ideas, occasions, etc.

3 Random word game

Using some of the team to create stimulus for the rest to work with

Step 1   2–4 people stand in a line with a leader facing them. The leader has created a list of pertinent words to the task in hand. The rest of the team watch ready to capture ideas.

Step 2   The leader says one of their pertinent words and points to one person in the line. They say the first associated word that comes into their head. The leader immediately points to someone else in the line and they have to say the first associated word that comes into their head.

Step 3   Keep repeating for 20 seconds or so then change to a new word. Watchers write down ideas that occur, stimulated by the random words that are thrown out.

This one sounds odd but it works very well to get 'out of the box' ideas.

4 Break category rules

When in a strong and large-scale category (e.g. laundry, pet food, cereal) this can help to break you out of convention and get you to fresh pastures.

Step 1   List all the rules of your category, spoken and unspoken, on to the left-hand side of a large flipchart page. List all the colours, shapes, names, sizes, benefits, communications and such like that typify the category.

Step 2   Go through the list and, one by one, break each rule using it to create a new idea.

In effect, Apple has done this consistently; making their computers friendly and colourful, not complex and beige.

5(a) Corporate takeover

This is a very powerful exercise and works well using case studies of successful brands.

Step 1   Choose 3–4 big successful brands who have achieved great things (e.g. Virgin, Nike, Gucci, Evian, etc.).

Step 2   In teams, take a brand and list the brand's key success factors.

Step 3   Now imagine that the management team of that brand has moved to run your brand in your category. They use the same vision and skill as in their old company. List the things they would do to grow.

5(b) Personality takeover

A version of the previous technique that pushes people further out of the box to find more extreme ideas.

Step 1   Choose 3–4 celebrity personalities in a particular strong role that everyone knows (e.g. Batman, Michael Douglas in Wall Street, Willy Wonka, Julie Andrews in the Sound of Music).

Step 2   In teams, chose a celebrity and list his/her qualities, character and values.

Step 3   Now imagine he/she is in charge of your brand. List what ideas he/she would come up with.

One might imagine that the folks at Caterpillar did this exercise with Imelda Marcos and ended up with shoes. But I don't think it happened that way!

6   Cross referencing

This is a very good technique for covering a lot of different angles in one exercise.

Step 1   Make a grid and populate the axes with different aspects of your brand (*x*-axis) and your target for innovation (*y*-axis).

Step 2   Cross reference to find easy fits and capture the obvious ideas.

Step 3   Force a connection between other elements that are not an easy fit and use this to create fresh ideas.

This is best explained via an example: Creating innovation ideas for Nescafé Gold Blend (see Figure 7.17).

7   Consumer immersion

This is very good as a stimulating break during a day long innovation workshop.

Step 1   Go to a relevant consumer hang out e.g. a bar, club, someone's home, a shopping centre, a restaurant . . . and *watch*.

Step 2   Compare notes and create ideas from what you've seen and discussed.

Be relevant: if you are working on a teen project, go to McDonald's or another teen hang out. If you are working in financial services then queue up in a bank at lunch time or meet up with an independent financial adviser.

8   Yes, and. . .

A great way to capture inspiration when it strikes.

Step 1   Give a post-it pad and a big marker pen to each team member. Get them to write down every thought they have as it occurs – one per post-it, only a couple of headline words on each. Stick all the post-its onto a flipchart and say them out loud, one by one.

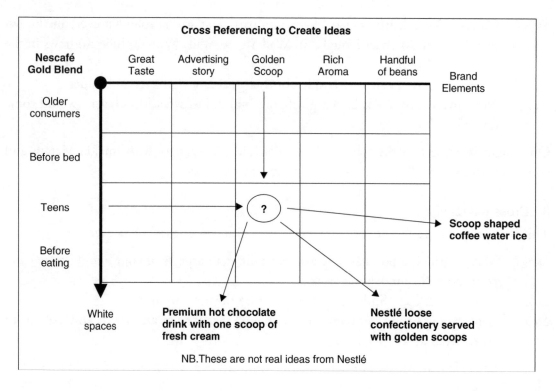

Figure 7.17: Innovation ideas for Nescafé Gold Blend/Special Filtre.

Step 2   Listen to the first person calling out his/her ideas and after each one add your own immediate thoughts (also on post-its) by thinking (in response to their idea) 'Yes, and also. . . (my idea)'. There can be no editing and no bad ideas. It should run very fast.

Step 3   When you have been round the group, stop, step back and summarize the good ideas.

9 Colours/Music

A very simple and useful exercise to get the creative juices flowing.

Step 1   Give everyone a colour and get them to write down all associations, feelings, moods, objects, etc., they can think of.

Step 2   Use these associations directly to create ideas.

A twist on this is to play a short snippet of music and ask everyone to react with associations and feelings then turn those into ideas. This can then be repeated for different styles of music.

10   Trend extrapolation

A very useful technique to use after a presentation or conference has thrown up a difficult or challenging theme or issue.

Step 1   Extrapolate the theme or issue; imagine that it takes hold and dominates. Capture all the general implications of this on consumer's lives, culture, society, etc.

Step 2   Turn each one of the implications into an idea.

An example might be for food ideas:

Interesting trend :	Aloe drinks in health shop
Extrapolation :	Aloe food in supermarkets, Aloe restaurants, Aloe addiction...
Food ideas :	Aloe-based diet snacks.

The brainstorming from Hell

Despite best intentions, brainstorming sessions can often be pretty uninspiring. Planning in the above techniques, peppered throughout the day, can liven any session up. What you certainly don't want to do is to end up in 'The Brainstorming from Hell' (see Box 7.1).

Box 7.1: The Brainstorming from Hell

- Get a large team of people from far and wide, more than 10, together in a small airless room with no windows
- Give them no clear brief, just "We're doing a brainstorming"
- Arrive late yourself
- No coffee or refreshments
- Don't do a warm-up
- Sit round a large U-shaped table
- Let people answer their mobiles throughout the session
- Spend 10 minutes explaining why this company simply can't come up with good ideas
- Have no agenda or process planned
- Get a junior team member to 'scribe' all ideas longhand onto a flipchart and keep flipping them over
- Kick it off with "come on then, give me some ideas"
- Verbally assassinate any idea that seems in any way odd or incomplete
- Leave early

Figure 7.18: Example of an Idea Sketch concept.

Ignition tools: types of concept and which to use

You've created lots of ideas using several different brainstorming techniques, but what is the best way to capture them? Marketers spend a lot of time in innovation processes talking about 'the concepts' and how they'll be tested/explored/refined, but not enough thought defining what type of concepts they need to be. Choosing the right concept format can really help to make things faster and clearer. But being too rigid with formats or getting too detailed too early can stifle creativity.

Here are five basic concept types. These are not exhaustive, and each category may require some different angles, but the principles they rest on are sound.

Concept type: Idea Sketch

- The basic concept (see Figure 7.18) captures the gist of an idea as it's created. It is very visual. In fact, sometimes early ideas are only visual, as the right words are just not there yet to capture the idea. Be comfortable with this.
- *When to use*: In an initial brainstorm session or 'quickie'.

Concept type: Core Concept

- The basic building block for any concept, it contains three essential components only (see Box 7.2):

Box 7.2: Example of a Core Concept (author's own)	
Name:	BREATHAWAY
Insight:	It means a lot to people when their dogs show their love by licking them, but a dog's bad breath can spoil it . . .
Benefit:	New Breath Away – the delicious crunchy dog biscuit that solves bad breath
Reason to Believe:	The unique formulation of parsley and eucalyptus leaves baked into the delicious crunchy biscuit neutralizes odours and freshens breath

- *Insight*: The consumer understanding that describes the need to be fulfilled
- *Benefit*: (sometimes called 'Proposition'): The key benefit the consumer gets from the product or service. This can be either functional or emotional or indeed both.
- *Reason to believe*: The proof we offer to support the benefit, in consumer relevant terms.

When to use:

- At the end of brainstorming sessions as the way to write up ideas.
- In early exploratory work with consumers.
- As part of more detailed concepts in later development work.

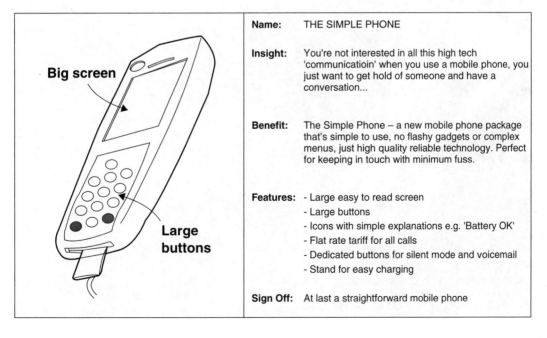

Figure 7.19: Example of a Technical Core Concept.

Concept type: Technical Core Concept

- When the idea comes from a technical source, or has its roots in a specific product feature, it is useful to reflect that in the style of the concept to capture the true essence of the idea.
- Features are added as more detailed reasons to believe, plus a sign off line to summarize the key offer (Figure 7.19).

When to use:

- As with Core Concepts, but when technical features play an important role and need to be interrogated individually as well as part of the whole.

Concept type: Adcept

- Creating a mock advert for print or outdoor can be an excellent way to bring a concept to life for consumers (see Figure 7.20).
- This requires graphic designers and/or creatives to be let loose with your ideas. This is not usually your advertising agency, but a design agency, then there is no confusion about whether this is real advertising: it isn't.

Figure 7.20: Example of an Adcept.

- The process of briefing creatives helps hugely in clarifying your thinking and so moves the idea forward.

When to use:

- When making changes to the personality, tone and style of a brand it can be very useful to mock up a full mix like this to feel where your ideas might take you.
- Use it in qualitative exploration, not in quantitative.
- It is important to focus on learning from this kind concept and not to evaluate it. Once again, it isn't advertising.

Concept type: Detailed

- This is a proforma concept that captures a great deal of detail (Box 7.3). It is based around the three core elements; insight, benefit and reasons to believe, and adds more elements to bring it closer to the brief for a full mix.

When to use:

- At later stages in idea development when you are seeking to finalize a concept.

Box 7.3: Example of a Detailed Concept (author's own)	
Name:	BREATH BUSTER
Brand:	Pedigree
Simple Desc:	Dog biscuits that tackle bad breath
Insight:	It means a lot to people when their dogs show their love by licking them, but a dog's bad breath can spoil it. . .
Proposition:	New Pedigree Breath Buster is the only delicious crunchy dog biscuit with Parsley and Eucalyptus that solves bad breath
Benefit:	Functional – Solves dog's bad breath – Healthy and delicious biscuit snack Emotional – I don't need to shy away when my dog shows we love
Features:	100% natural, rice and biscuit snack Eucalyptus freshens breath Parsley neutralizes odours in the stomach
Other RTB:	From Pedigree, Top Breeders recommend it
Tone/style:	Consistent with rest of Pedigree Snacks and Treats range
Target:	Dog owners who notice their dog's bad breath and hesitate on getting close
Source of Gains:	Other standard dog biscuits including Pedigree offers
Pricing:	Sold at a premium to standard dog biscuits
Key Occasion:	Regular – 'Treat time' every day Specific – Before family time when we all get close
Picture:	[Attached]

7.3   3 BUCKET PRINCIPLE

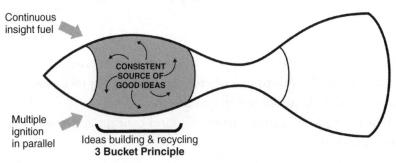

Getting three buckets may not sound at first to be the obvious answer to an innovation process problem, but this is a simple principle that has been used to great effect on many large innovation projects. From the diagrams it can look a little complex, but in practice it's really quite easy to do. It is a flexible way to capture and manage all the ideas you create in a project. No major IT system or relational database is needed, just a few folders and some pluck.

What it is

It is an idea management system that is very simple. There are three buckets or receptacles of any kind in which to keep all ideas created by the team. A4 'In trays' or foolscap folders work well, but getting a set of real buckets may make a bolder statement about changing the way ideas are managed.

Bucket 1   ALL ideas you create go in here. Never throw any away.
Bucket 2   Ideas that show promise are moved to Bucket 2.
Bucket 3   Ideas that seem to have real potential – those you are most excited by – are put into Bucket 3.

By simply using these three buckets to manage the ideas you produce, it can have a major impact on the quantity and quality of ideas you have to work with. Use them in brainstorming sessions, whole projects, across different projects and throughout everything you do in the year.

Bucket loads of ideas

To kick start a new Bucket system, go large – get yourself a huge bucket (a plastic dustbin in a fun colour will do) and plonk it right in the middle of your department. Instruct

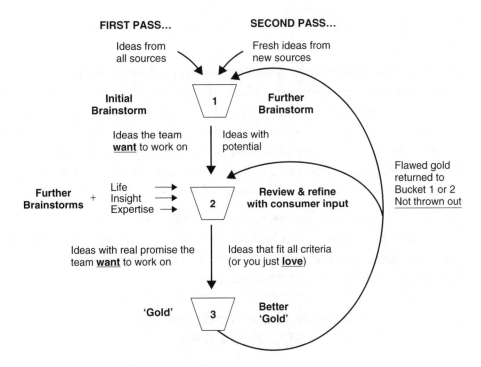

FIRST PASS... **SECOND PASS...**

Ideas from all sources

Fresh ideas from new sources

Initial Brainstorm **1** **Further Brainstorm**

Ideas the team **want** to work on

Ideas with potential

Further Brainstorms + Life Insight Expertise → **2** **Review & refine with consumer input**

Flawed gold returned to Bucket 1 or 2 Not thrown out

Ideas with real promise the team **want** to work on

Ideas that fit all criteria (or you just **love**)

'Gold' **3** **Better 'Gold'**

Figure 7.21: The 3 Bucket Principle: how it works.

everyone to put any ideas they have and all outputs from sessions, chats, debriefs, etc., onto A4 sheets and put them in the bucket. Assign someone to be the Bucket Monitor and ask that person to empty and file everything in a folder neatly once a week. You can then stick the number of ideas collected on a large sign on the side of the bucket to show people how creative they are being. You can even track it to evaluate your team's creativity, if you feel so moved.

How it works in practice (Figure 7.21)

FIRST PASS

Step 1 All ideas generated for a project go into Bucket 1. This includes existing ideas, old concepts, previously rejected ideas, boring, stupid, naïve and incomplete ideas – this is where the maxim 'there's no such thing as a bad idea' works well – it's all useful grist to the mill.

Step 2 Work through all these ideas, discuss them, build them up, combine them and play with them until some start to gleam a bit brighter than the rest, generating excitement and energy in the team. Take these promising ideas in their new form and put them into Bucket 2.

BUT   *Do not throw away any of the remaining ideas. Keep them in Bucket 1.*

Step 3   Work through these promising ideas adding insight and expertise as you see fit – maybe a round of qualitative research, a trawl through the R&D department, a chat with a child psychologist ... whatever adds value to the idea in your overall process. Also, start bringing your ideas to life at this point. Theatre rules need to start applying here. As you build and refine the ideas, some will start emerging into real potential – this is your **gold**: proceed with these to Bucket 3.

BUT   *Do not throw away any of the remaining ideas. Keep them in Bucket 2.*

Step 4   Once you have a Bucket 3 that has some *gold* in it, it is tempting to stop, but this is only the beginning of the real power in the 3 Bucket Principle. You now go back to the start and begin to create fresh ideas again.

> # You are now ready for the SECOND PASS

Step 1   Start again. Go back to your source material/innovation platforms/insight pillars and create new ideas. This forces your process to push further into new territories, edges of the map you hadn't been to before. Put all these ideas into Bucket 1 and mix and meld them again – combining first and second round ideas together. Maybe there's a little thought that went nowhere in the first round but now, connected to a strong new idea, it suddenly has real legs. Take everything with promise to Bucket 2

BUT   *Still keep hold of everything left in Bucket 1.*

Step 2   Repeat as in the first rounds. Add insight, experts, technical know-how, consumer input – whatever brings value and deepens understanding. Bring ideas to life with pictures, examples, even rough mock-ups. Again you will have ideas emerging with real potential. These maybe the same ones as before, now stronger and better, or totally new ideas, but each will have been improved as it passes through each bucket. The ideas you now take to Bucket 3 are starting to look more like *solid gold*.

This is a process you can repeat again and again until you have only genuine *gold* in Bucket 3. It can be done very quickly – all in a day – or steadily through the course of a full innovation project. It is designed to work as the ideas management framework for any innovation project. Here is a real example from my time at Added Value (Figure 7.22).

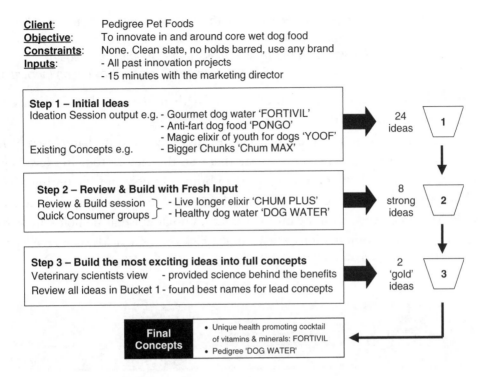

Figure 7.22: 3 Bucket example: A Dog's Breakfast.

Results

A year later the 'FORTIVIL' ingredient was in every can of Pedigree Chum around the world as part of a major global relaunch.

Pedigree 'DOG WATER' was trialled and shelved due to perceived lack of a market for it. The team felt the timing was wrong . . . but who knows when the time will be right for this idea? If you think it's a stupid idea that will **never** get off the ground, then you should have a look at the website for a Californian company *www.k9waterco.com* and maybe pick up a litre of their chicken-flavoured toilet water for dogs – it's 'Rebarkably Refreshing^{TM}'. No, really.

Grave-robbing

The 3 Bucket Principle allows you very easily to indulge in a spot of grave-robbing. That is, stealing ideas from the past to improve what you know today. It has been a tried and trusted route for such great men as Leonardo da Vinci. Huge insights and inspiration can be gained from looking at the anatomy of previous work. Two academics, Andrew Hargadon and Robert I. Sutton, spent five years studying businesses that innovate constantly:

'We learned two big things. The first is that the best innovators systematically use old ideas as the raw materials for one new idea after another... (the second is) the companies we studied have found out how to make that leap again and again.'

Source: Harvard Business Review on Innovation

Ben & Jerry's is a serial innovator and proudly display their 'flavours that never made it' to the public on their website in their 'Flavor Graveyard' (Figure 7.23).

Where other companies would hide their failures and 'silly' ideas in shame, Ben & Jerry's show them off with pride. You can even taste them on the factory tour in New England. They see it as a mark of their continuing quest to bring you new and interesting ice cream recipes. I believe that it also serves as a very powerful vault of ideas to inspire them in creating the next 'Phish Food'. Anyone in the business is left in no doubt that no holds are barred in the search for new taste combinations when a quick flick through yields such excellent failed flavours as 'Makin' Whoopee Pie', 'Fudge Behaving Badly' and 'Karamel Sutra'.

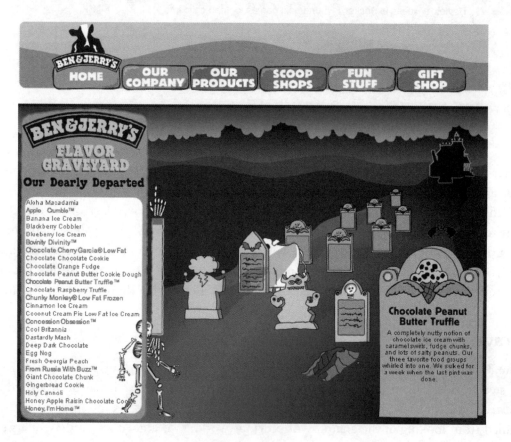

Figure 7.23: Ben & Jerry's Flavor Graveyard.

> ## Stop reinventing the past and start using it as fuel for the future

Keeping your Bucket 1 and 2 concepts and ideas between innovation projects and thus using them as the kindling to start your next innovation fire is a simple way to be an effective grave-robber and get the maximum from all the resources that go into creating and building ideas.

A word on innovation intranets and databases

It is a sound principle to keep old concepts and make them totally accessible globally and to back them up so that nothing is ever lost. This is why many businesses attempt to capture and store old concepts in their company intranets.

It never works.

At McKinsey, the globally renowned strategy consultants, they have an enviable record for leveraging their collected knowledge. But the team tasked with designing the knowledge management system found that simply digitizing the information and making it easily accessible to everyone didn't work. People didn't bother searching through a relational database to see if there was any useful data to help them. What the team discovered is that people were looking for something more than data. They were also looking for inspiration. What they designed instead was a 'who knows what' directory that is constantly updated. The Rapid Response Team, as it is now known, promises to link anyone, within 24 hours, to others who might have useful knowledge. This process puts people in touch with the thinking and ideas in their original format; a person. Likewise in innovation, there is something about handwritten or original format concepts that capture their moment of glory, their 15 minutes of fame when they were hot. Putting them into the clothes of a common proforma and making them uniform in size and shape just seems to kill them dead – like seedlings over watered. I have nothing against the global accessibility principle, and I hope someone cracks it one day, but keeping the concepts in original physical format (photocopiable, of course) has my vote.

Fresh ideas are analogue, don't digitize them when they are too young.

7.4   CODA: A WHOLE YEAR VIEW OF INNOVATION

In pursuit of the most effective way to create ideas in a typical marketing department with several brands and products and a range of different ongoing innovation challenges, it is worth looking at the whole year of work as an ideation process in itself. Wouldn't it be great if, without much planning or extra resource, you could get a continuous source of new ideas all through the year? This does not mean setting off a never-ending brainstorming session, but creating a rich seam of ideas within your team that is continually bubbling up with new thoughts on all aspects of the mix as well as being directed towards particular areas when the need arises. This is entirely possible and practical. Let us look at 3M.

The 15% rule

3M insist that their staff give 15% of their time to 'free' innovation. That means that they work on personal hunches, unofficial projects and are given access to almost anything they can lay their hands on. They are constantly looking for new ideas and they therefore look at any situation or group of people as a potential source of tomorrow's big idea. At a recent conference a marketer from 3M was talking about innovation and showed how deep the 'anytime is ideas time' mantra was when he presented a new technology that allows light to be bent round curves in high-tech 'light pipes'; he asked us to please get in contact if we could think of a good application for this idea – none had yet been found! This continuous approach to ideation means that they have a tremendous record of outstanding innovation across many fields.

Your typical year

Consider a typical year of innovation in a busy local, regional or global marketing team (Figure 7.24): a couple of major innovation projects, new team members joining, conferences, agency presentations, tracking studies, inputs of all types from all directions that could be useful for creating ideas. But the cumulative effect of all those inputs is not usually turned into ideas.

Two techniques to help you to get more from what you already do

To create a continuous flow of ideas in your team it helps to add a couple of techniques into your array of innovation approaches. These are simple and easy to implement. When put

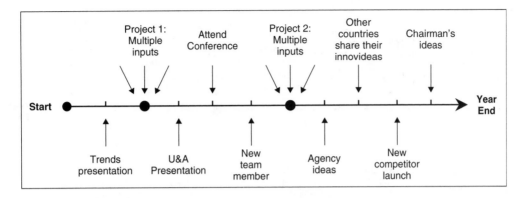

Figure 7.24: A typical year of innovation inputs.

into practice they will help you to generate more quality ideas from the work you already do – a very cost-effective and efficient use of time and resources.

- *Brainstorming 'quickies'*
  At each input moment do a short sharp impromptu brainstorming session. Irrespective of whether you have a detailed brief worked up – do a quickie. If not, invent a brief that works well enough for the moment to give some direction, for example:
  - How do we target X (non-traditional target)
  - Reinvent core product to be half size/cost/time
  - Revisit your last major innovation brief.

  After every presentation you receive – be it a research debrief, a competitor review or even a conference paper – gather your team and spend 10 – 20 minutes generating ideas. Capture them any way that's handy and then add them into your Bucket 1 set of general ideas as source material for any and all projects you are pursuing.

- *Ideas amnesty*
  Once (or twice – your call) a year, hold an Ideas Amnesty session. Rather like a knife amnesty, but the inverse, as you are seeking people to turn in their hidden treasures rather than their dangerous obsessions. Invite your team to bring all those ideas that got away; those tucked away in desk drawers or lying unspoken in timid hearts must surface and be counted. You should offer no judgement in what you accept – all ideas are welcome, irrespective of source. You could consider extending the invitation to your agencies, colleagues, researchers, bosses, R&D, indeed anyone with knowledge of the brands and category you're in. Get all the ideas out in the open in an informal session, and give all the ideas a ranking. It is also essential that you use the time to put them together to see if any new initiatives are sparked. Don't just evaluate them singly.

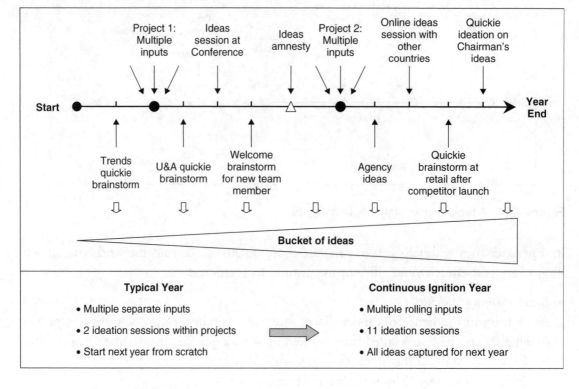

Figure 7.25: Continuous Ignition year.

Putting these two simple techniques into practice across your department can create a remarkable effect: Your year's innovation work, previously a disjointed assemblage of fairly random events, now becomes a continuous stream of ideas (see Figure 7.25), building cumulative power with each new input.

With little extra effort or resources you can achieve **10 times** the quantity of ideas and be confident of higher quality because the ideas combine together and build.

Key takeouts

1 Pushing to source insights from far and wide, off the beaten track, to get a full 360° perspective deepens your understanding and uncovers more opportunities.
2 Running different ideation sessions in parallel greatly increases both the quality and quantity of ideas you create.

3 Designing each ideation process and session differently, to fit the task better, will yield richer results.

4 Using relevant concept templates for each stage of the idea creation and development process helps to keep ideas at their most powerful throughout.

5 Thinking of your year not as a series of discrete projects but as a continuous process of insight and ideation will help to increase your innovation effectiveness.

Checklist: Combustion

	YES	NO
• Is insight into your key innovation projects genuinely coming from all over – a full 360° perspective?	☐	☐
• Do you run separate brainstorming sessions, with different kinds of people, in parallel?	☐	☐
• Do your brainstorming sessions each feel different and specific?	☐	☐
• Do you use different concept types at different stages?	☐	☐
• Do you keep all your ideas, however dumb, from project to project?	☐	☐
• Do you run quickie brainstorms after conference papers or presentations on brand tracking, trends, etc.?	☐	☐

 Handover

We have looked in detail at how to generate enough good-quality ideas for each of your innovation projects. The next stage is to tackle the thorny issue of getting all these great ideas down to the few to work up in detail. How to do this process without taking ages and spending an arm and a leg on evaluative research? The Nozzle stage of Rocketing takes a different view from the testing heavy processes beloved by current funnel methodologies. For swift and efficient prioritization that's fun, read on.

Rocketing: Nozzle

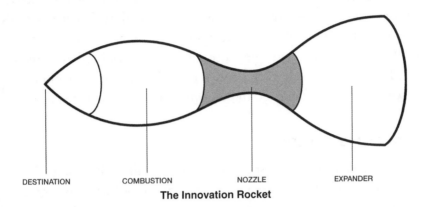

CHAPTER 8

DESTINATION   COMBUSTION   NOZZLE   EXPANDER

The Innovation Rocket

 ## Headlines

How to get lots of good ideas down to a few great ideas is one of the toughest bits of innovation to get right. Performing rather than presenting ideas, together with prototyping and visualization, brings them to life and thus gives the best chance of showing their true potential. By combining objective evaluation criteria and gut instinct based on experience, prioritization of the best ideas can be done more accurately and much more swiftly than in the standard funnel stage-gate process.

From Whittle to 'Wow'

Now that you have 'bucket' loads of simply wonderful ideas in your project you need to reduce them to the one or two on which it is worth spending real time and money to develop. This is perhaps the toughest bit of innovation. As outlined in Chapter 4, the standard stage-gate process makes this a very slow, expensive and painful process with no real guarantee (judging by the results) that you do actually pick the winner. Consumers tend to opt for the more familiar or easier ideas and can ignore the really good but challenging ones in quantitative concept tests. So can it be done differently, and better? To increase your success levels and decrease your stress levels you need to act much more like the Nozzle in a rocket motor:

> A quick and ruthless contraction of a large volume to a small powerful core with tremendous power

The analogy of gases being pressurized down to fit through a small venturi nozzle creating tremendous thrust, is a good one. It implies a fast process that forces ideas together, creating better quality lead ideas with high impact. That means that the usual reductive 'whittling down' becomes instead a process that adds value to your ideas. To achieve this you need some objective evaluation tools that can incorporate all points of view, not just consumer concept tests. To facilitate this you must also give your ideas the best possible chance to shine at this early stage in their development. Rather than just trot them out as paragraphs on a blank PowerPoint chart, you need to perform them as if you were on stage.

Picking winners is a lottery

Do you ever feel that innovation is just like the lottery; loads of hope and wishful thinking, but the reality is that you have a one in a million chance of hitting it big? The process of turning a sieve load of ideas into a few golden nuggets is fraught with difficulty. Marketers have got themselves into a rut. There are two key reasons why we make whittling down to the big ideas a long drawn-out uncertain process:

1. *We get lost in PowerPoint* – poor internal screening
2. *We delegate the task to consumers to decide for us* – poor external screening.

How should we tackle these two demons of the innovation world? One word will do. . .

Showbusiness

We need to get more 'show' into the business of innovation. Ideas are about inspiration, newness, excitement and ultimately a performance, where they go on show to the consumer for the first time. By taking a leaf from the entertainment industry and increasing the wow-factor of our ideas in development, we can dramatically improve them and their chances of finding success. Also, by relying more on gut instinct and experience in making important decisions, less time and money need be spent entrusting them to consumers alone. That means getting good ideas launched more quickly and with less money spent in development.

Yo! – a rebel story

Simon Woodroffe cuts a unique business figure atop his burgeoning Yo! empire. He is not a briefcase-carrying venture capital leveraging business *wunderkind*, nor is he a careful artisan crafting his life's ambition. He's a sideburn toting, rockabilly maverick. And he knows how to put the 'show' into 'business'. His accomplishments are a growing chain of innovative sushi restaurants in the UK, Yo! Sushi, and a new category of budget boutique hotel, Yotel, soon to pop up in international airports (Figure 8.1). He also has various other business ventures in germination that will extend his success still further. His route to this point is in no way conventional.

He didn't go to university, preferring life as a roadie in the rock world. This developed by chance into him becoming a stage designer for rock gigs, culminating in the design for Live Aid, possibly the largest rock concert the world has ever seen. After that he went looking for something new. He tried his hand at a few things – coffee machines, property and other random ideas that took his fancy. On one particular jaunt to Japan, chasing after another spur of the moment deal, he saw a conveyor belt Sushi restaurant. "That would be cool in the UK" he thought. So he blagged himself a large mortgage and bought a dishevelled shop in the wrong part of Soho. By robbing Peter to pay Paul and having a way of convincing suppliers to trust him, he built his first Yo! Sushi – inventing unique features along the way such as on tap still and sparkling water at each table, remote control drinks trolleys and buttons that shout "Yo!" when you want service. All of these he brought in because he thought they would be cool. His passion for consumer service, flair and sheer bloody mindedness brought it all together into a strong coherent offer. Timing and luck did the rest – Marks & Spencer launched their own sushi lunch trays and other retailers followed suit, 'tipping' sushi into the mainstream for the first time. Soho was regenerated with the new media crowd hungry for something new, and *voila!*, a growth phenomenon was born.

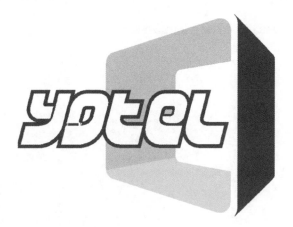

Figure 8.1: The next Yo! innovation – YoTel.

Most recently Simon was seen on TV as a millionaire looking for entrepreneurial ideas for investment in the popular series 'Dragon's Den' in the UK. Ordinary people pitch their own inventions to five investor 'Dragons' in the hope that they'll convince them to put up backing money there and then. In the show he is pugnacious, passionate and unpredictable: a consummate innovator.

If we look at two sides of Showbusiness in Figure 8.2 and apply them to innovation, we get two useful principles which address the key issues head on:

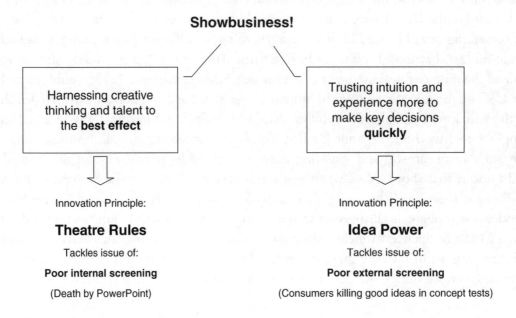

Figure 8.2: It's a crazy idea but it just might work. . . .

POOR INTERNAL SCREENING

Death by powerpoint

'It's the first time we've expressed the benefit using the word "best" instead of "better". *We're very excited.'* We've all been there, the dingy room at the end of the corridor, overcrowded and underlit, you stare at the wall in silence. 'This one's a real move forward' announces the young marketer as he clicks to yet another seemingly identical concept typed on a plain background.

And this is innovation?

The simple truth is that we use PowerPoint too much in innovation work. We drown in it. We are looking for inspiration, insight, excitement and newness yet restrict ourselves 90% of the time to the same tools we use for the quarterly budget meeting. Why?

Mobile Madness

I have cold shivers running down my spine as I recall the time I wrote a series of innovation concepts for a large telecoms client. I was working with a senior planner in a top global agency, a New Yorker through and through. He had awesome word firepower and he wasn't afraid to use it. We put all the ingenuity, insight, guile and wordplay we had into those concepts. We spent 48 hours straight crafting and refining them into the proforma required for presenting to the global market team.

The result? What do you think? We showed a whole host of concepts distinguished only by a 1 × 2 inch picture of a person holding a phone in a slightly different way. They died. And so did many other great ideas—ideas that are still being reinvented and launched today more than two years later.

If only we had ignored the proforma, turned off the PowerPoint and performed the ideas we really felt passionate about.

Show business: Theatre Rules

The principle is simple: treat innovation concept presentations, reviews, status meetings (in fact any time you have to share ideas) as a theatrical performance.

When putting on a play or musical the actors don't just turn up at the allotted time, wearing their everyday clothes, and just read out the lines standing against a plain background with fixed lighting and no movement. Nor should you when sharing ideas. If you want your audience to get excited and involved and share your passion then **perform** your ideas!

Theatre rules are good discipline for any evaluation. Having a common format for ideas to be evaluated makes common sense, but in my view it does not equal a level playing field. What it does instead is drag everything down to the lowest common denominator, obscuring the value that some ideas have and others do not. There are better ways to drive commonality in evaluation: same amount of resources in developing mock-ups, same time allocated for presentation, or using the same retail layout in which to communicate your ideas.

The Wizard of Oz

Streets is Unilever's Ice Cream business in Australia and in 2001 had a serious need for some profitable innovation – fast. The new marketing director embarked on an ambitious project to invent ideas across all the brands and to push his team to find new value chains, business systems and categories to exploit. He hired Added Value, where I was MD, as his innovation agency and involved his whole department along with technical, sales and manufacturing representatives – a bold move but one that achieved the galvanizing effect he was after. Very soon concepts for day-crèches, kids' clothing, alcoholic drinks and family fun cafés were knocking about the team causing a lot of excitement. All well and good, but he realized that the impending presentation to the senior management team would not be a smooth ride unless the ideas were whittled down to achievable concepts that had some business substance behind them. Yet he did not want to call a halt to the creative enthusiasm he had unleashed. Working together we devised a method to keep both creativity and business logic to the fore: we created an 'investors' panel' and set up a big pitch for the concepts.

The 'investors' panel' comprised the marketing director, the senior sales and manufacturing representatives, as well as some wise external heads – the MD of a trusted research agency and the planner from their global ad agency. Each concept idea was assigned a two-person team who were given a 15-minute slot, with 15 minutes for questions. Suddenly conceptual ideas began taking three-dimensional shape as the teams found props, made mock-ups, even hired in costumes and wrote scripts in their bid to win over the investment dollars in the panel's pockets. Each team knew they had to be succinct and to the point and give an idea of business return for their ideas as well as capture the hearts of the panel with their creativity and positive use of brand equity.

There is nothing like an impending performance for focusing the mind. What resulted was far different from a standard PowerPoint run through of a dozen concepts – it was an exhilarating show. The panel had a simple set of criteria and were able to choose the best ideas having seen them given as much life as was humanly possible in the time – the best way to judge ideas.

Here are some simple, practical Theatre Rules to use in every innovation project:

Theatre Rule 1

Prototype: Create a rough product, make a mock-up, visualize your idea.

Do more prototyping and less concept writing. It's that simple. No one ever fell in love with a one paragraph description of someone else. You need to see them in the flesh. A picture is worth a thousand words, and a prototype is worth a million more. People react more truthfully and directly to visual and physical stimulus – it's why we spend so much time and money on our packaging. This is no different in internal idea screening sessions. Why when marketers walk into an airless room with a laptop and a projector do we suddenly expect them to change into 2-D only simpletons? We give them page after page of slightly differently worded paragraphs and expect them to see instantly all the subtle differences. We need to present prototypes, images, mock-ups or even example objects to give a truer more useful representation of our ideas. At L'Oreal, when a new concept is presented to the boss, no PowerPoint is allowed, none. All he wants to see is a prototype or mock-up. If the idea cannot be captured in pack and graphics then it won't get across to consumers, however cleverly the concept is worded.

Music to the eyes

At Vodafone the team tasked with developing their download music offer had a good strategy presentation ready to show their boss. Their idea was to set up in-store demo stations so that people could actually experience the quality of music available through mobile downloads before signing up. Great on paper, but they were worried it wouldn't get the go-ahead as it would inevitably throw up many questions. They knew that the pressure was on to have a winner that would generate sign-ups in-store immediately. They decided to bring their strategy to life. They worked with their in-store merchandising agency to develop a fully functioning and branded music download demo 'pod' that could go in a real store. They took decisions and developed the best solution they knew how. Come the day of the meeting they had the fully functioning prototype installed in their boss's office. The presentation was simple – "Here it is". He loved it. In fact, he loved it so much that it was rolled out to thousands of stores across Europe.

Theatre Rule 2

Set the Scene: Choose somewhere that has the right ambience for enthusiasm. Sofas, natural light, great coffee – it's all important!

This could be your first date with the rest of your career – get the mood right! For some businesses it's a must to get outside the office. Many Starbucks have excellent sit and chat areas in their less busy downstairs/upstairs rooms. For others it's a dark room or a cinema. Wherever you can get real focus on the ideas and the emotional room for people to get excited about them, that's your spot.

Home cooking

When preparing for the debrief on a food innovation project to a large multinational brand owner I was concerned that the big idea we had developed would fall on somewhat stony ground. We needed to get the client team into the consumer's world for them to really appreciate our thinking – not because it was complex or far-out, quite the opposite, because it was so simple. Theirs was a cook-in-sauce brand and the idea we had for their pasta bake range was that you could make it without pre-cooking the pasta. Not earth shattering innovation, but a real time saving for their core consumers – people for whom 'home cooking' meant opening a packet and heating up it in the microwave. We turned our meeting room into a kitchen. We hired in a cooker, borrowed a microwave, bought a roll of cheap linoleum flooring and brought in our own pots & pans. We started the meeting by cooking everyone breakfast. When it came to the main event, we gathered everyone round the kitchen table and demonstrated the benefit by cooking pasta for lunch. No PowerPoint, maximum impact.

Theatre Rule 3

Use props: Bring examples from other categories. Use physical objects to make your point.

Have you ever seen a one-man show and marvelled at how, with just a scarf, a chair or a hat stand, an actor can create a whole scene in vivid technicolor? When it's 5pm the day before a 9am concept meeting, don't spend your last hour fiddling with animation in PowerPoint, go out and buy some props!

   If you're talking about laxatives, then bring in a toilet roll, or even a toilet. Even if it's online financial services, then having the back of an A4 envelope with scribbled numbers and a chewed pen will help to create a scene in which your idea can mean something. When working with Prudential to invent their online financial services brand egg, the Added Value team made team made cheque books, credit cards and bank statements with the name on them – before any design work had been done – so that when presenting the idea to the board they would be able to visualize it and not just stare at a word on a blank PowerPoint chart. The board hated the name, but they saw the potential and signed it off.

Theatre Rule 4

Tell a story: Don't just hit your audience directly with an idea, work up to it. Weave a story that delivers the central idea in a way that makes it feel right.

Victor Hugo could have just said 'We should treat the poor better', but instead he wrote *Les Miserables* to give his idea a better chance to be accepted. You don't have to write an epic but even if you are presenting a concept for dog biscuits, start with 'the little girl on the sofa with her dog . . .' and your idea will find more fertile ground.

A winning story

When at my previous company Added Value, we had a major pitch to the global innovation team of a FTSE 100 client. The stakes were high so a top team was gathered and we worked for a solid week developing a cutting edge innovation proposal. It was laden with process diagrams, detailed explanations, examples from other categories – everything that you could put into a PowerPoint presentation was thrown in. Then we re-read the brief and realized that our pitch was only one hour, including discussion, and it was to be held on HMS *Belfast*, an old WWII battleship moored on the Thames. Projecting PowerPoint was therefore going to be difficult and, moreover, if they were going as far as to hire a battleship, surely they were expecting more than just a slideshow? We decided to stick to our guns, shorten the document and have a rehearsal on Friday afternoon in front of some of the other directors. It was an unqualified disaster. Long, unfocused and boring. 'We thought you were supposed to be dazzling them with your creativity and inventiveness?' We needed a major rethink. Over the weekend the realization dawned that we had been approaching it all wrong. They didn't want process and detail, they wanted us to show our thinking and inspire them, to take them on a journey. The only way to take people on an inspiring journey without leaving the room was to tell them a story. So the pitch became a short story. The team pounced on it on Monday morning and 24 short hours later they had turned it into a hard bound A3 story book, beautifully laid out with images and illustrations. Here is how it opened:

Foreword

This is a story about creativity with a purpose, it has laughter, tears, moments of triumph and moments of despair and even a fire-breathing dragon, but above all it has people working together towards a burning goal.

It starts with two men, an Arabic-speaking restaurant critic and a French lawyer, who are discussing their childhood ...

When we wanted to bring in an example of the power of great ideas, we chose OMO, Unilever's global detergent brand, and it's new brand idea 'Dirt Is Good' that flies in the face of conventional 'war against stains' thinking. We wrote it as a story, based on the relaunched brand's performance in a tough market ...

The Child, the Paintbrush and the Dragon

In Pakistan, a devout Muslim country, OMO was really in trouble. It was on the Unilever death list. The team were in despair.

P&G were spending more than twice their budget on TV and had dropped their prices by 50%. An insurmountable foe.

A fire-breathing dragon.

So three people – the brand manager and two others – decided to throw themselves into Dirt Is Good and throw everything else out. They put their entire budget (all of it) into one event – a kids' painting party.

They started in one city with local radio and cheap TV to promote the event on the outskirts of town. 2000 mums and kids showed up.

They went to the next town, and the next, relentlessly. They didn't see their families or take a moment off for 3 months.

By no. 60 they had 20 000 turning up. In the big cities they caused gridlock. By the end, over 600 000 people had been involved, including the Education Minister and the Guinness Book of World Records.

OMO overtook Ariel to take the no. 1 spot at twice the price, with half the spend.

The dragon was slain.

The pitch was 'a revelation' and we won the business, or in the client's words, we 'left all the other agencies far far behind'. Did we have cleverer people? Maybe. Did we have a better process? Probably not. What we did was to bring our thinking to life in an inspiring and original way – we told a story.

Theatre Rule 5

Rehearse: Practice presenting your ideas.

Even if this is the only rule you obey in your next innovation project – it will pay dividends. Get your team to use their partners at home, or even that nice chap in purchasing, as a test audience. The pitch rehearsal is a permanent fixture in ad agencies. They know that without a rehearsal with all their boards, props, videos and a full team, they will not do their best in front of their prospective client. What are ad agencies selling? Ideas. The only difference between you presenting an innovation concept to your boss and a new ad agency presenting their communications idea to your boss is budget and clothing (in advertising there seems to be a rule for pitches: you can wear anything you like, as long as it's a black suit). You are both selling ideas just the same, so a little practice goes a long way.

The turning point in the Added Value pitch was the rehearsal in front of the other directors. The act of getting up and presenting our ideas in real time brought many issues immediately to the fore. It inspired us to go away and completely rethink our approach. It can be an embarrassing thing to do, but much better to squirm and struggle in front of a friendly audience who are there to help than when presenting for real.

The Theatre Rules are summarized in Box 8.1.

Box 8.1: Summary of Theatre Rules	
Prototype	Draw a picture, make a mock-up, use imagery. Pictures communicate faster than words. Use them.
Set the scene	Get the right ambience for presenting ideas. Go to a coffee shop. Change the lighting. Mood matters.
Use props	Bring examples from other categories. Show what others have achieved to enhance your ideas.
Tell a story	Warm them up. Draw them in. This is innovation foreplay.
Rehearse	Try it all out. Get some feedback. Learn your opening line.

POOR EXTERNAL SCREENING

Consumers killing good ideas

Market research is a double-edged sword: remarkably good for slicing through to the key issues and opportunities where used correctly, and incredibly good at killing ideas at birth if mishandled. In many cases research has simply been allowed to take over, replacing marketing judgement and strategic vision. Average everyday consumers have, in effect, evaluated the tender new ideas and found them wanting and marketers take their word for it. It's good to get to the 'why' behind consumer reaction – why did they like it; why didn't they like it? – but it must be understood in context.

In quantitative research, particularly, the consumer scores are taken as fact and ideas that score poorly are thrown out leaving only a few behind as 'winners'. Ideas in a typical innovation process are usually not strong enough to withstand close scrutiny, they have no real 'mix' around them to convince consumers of their validity, so consumers are not judging reality. Their reactions should be inputs to *help us to learn* and develop the ideas, not simply go/no go decisions.

Show business: Idea Power

This is a simple idea: one that you can implement immediately on ongoing projects. It is very powerful in its clarity and impact. It does not replace consumer input but incorporates it more meaningfully.

Rather than attempt to judge if an idea is a winner or has legs by asking consumers for an evaluative thumbs up or thumbs down, Idea Power is a way to give an idea a meaningful ranking that focuses on its potential drawn from a number of different criteria. By focusing on the idea rather than the concept, it is hoped that there will be less incentive to ditch poor scorers and more to ask the question 'How can this idea be strengthened?'.

Experience and Evaluation Combined

Consumers are not very sensitive to new ideas. They have no qualms about killing them stone dead if they show the slightest weakness. We don't want to pander to poor ideas, but bringing in experience rather than just cold evaluation on its own, can give you the best of both worlds; the benefit of knowing how the category works, or how much impact on consumers a new channel will have can greatly sway how much potential an idea has. Give it straight to consumers on a piece of A4 and it's too easy for them not to get it first time. They are, after all, not marketers.

By acting on Theatre Rules and bringing ideas to life – giving them three dimensions of reality – you can then get a much better read on your views and see where the team's passion lies. It may be that the idea is still buried in the concept and has yet to be eked out correctly. With prototyping and visualization this will be more apparent to the experienced marketer.

The Idea Power approach combines both these elements to give you a balanced prioritization, quickly.

How it works

Its basis is a weighted average matrix. First you select a number of criteria to judge your idea on (normally between 4 and 5). Give each of these a weighting according to their importance for your specific situation. Score each idea against each criteria. Create a matrix of the scores. The total of these scores is the **Idea Power**.

The right criteria

Choosing the right criteria is of course critical, but experience shows that there are a few criteria that make more sense to use than others. These should be your core criteria and should be balanced between those that require experienced judgement and those that can be more objectively measured (Table 8.1). There are also specific items that are pertinent to the project in hand. In total a practical matrix should have around 4–6 criteria: fewer and there is no real value in the combination, more and it becomes complex to use in a group

Table 8.1: Idea Power criteria.

Criteria	Explanation	Scoring
Fit to brand	Does it deliver on your brand vision?	Hi, Med, Lo
Consumer appeal	Do consumers love it?	Hi, Med, Lo
Relevant differentiation	How different & better do consumers see it vs competition?	Hi, Med, Lo
Feasibility	How easy is it to do?	Easy, Hard, Very hard
Expertise required	Does your business have the skills to deliver this idea	In team, In company, Buy in
Investment	How much would it cost to be able to make this?	Hi, Med, Lo
Global applicability	How many markets is this applicable to?	Local only, A few, Most
Margin	How much money will this generate for us, per unit?	Hi, Med, Lo
Passion	How excited are you by this idea?	Hi, Med, Lo

conversation and fits better to a more detailed desk analysis of an idea (that may very well be relevant at a later stage of development, but not at this early stage).

Criteria options

Fit to brand

Does the idea align with your brand positioning, values or equities? This works very well when delivering to a new brand vision as it helps bring the sometimes dry words of a vision to life when connecting them to a new product or service.

Consumer appeal

This is where consumer feedback makes its entry. Be it qualitative feedback from a research debrief or top box scores from a concept screener, they can fit into the matrix in their proper place without overpowering all else. This can also be a measure of your teams gut feel as to consumer appeal – or even that gut feel augmented by chatting to only a couple of consumers or secretaries. Each of these inputs has validity and can be weighted accordingly.

Relevant differentiation

How different is this idea to the competitive set, for the target consumers? Second only to Passion, this is a 'killer criterion'. Too often used only as 'differentiation', it can be misused appallingly. Products and services that are just different may divert you for a few moments but will not gain your loyalty and trust, as any consumer will tell you (but most probably by saying 'it's OK' in a focus group). Differentiation must be relevant to pack a punch; relevant to the consumer and the need they have. This is sometimes a difficult one to judge without some consumer feedback. As marketers, deeply immersed in our product, category and innovation project, concepts can seem extremely differentiated from one another. It is only when you show them to consumers that you find you have been dancing on the head of a pin and ordinary people see no differences at all. This is an acid test for any idea. Part of it's potency as a criterion is that it can stand for any aspect of the mix. This is not confined to benefits or substantiation of those benefits, but can cover packaging, distribution, added services, values, price – anything that makes it different and better than the rest in a way that a consumer would value. If you have no consumer feedback of any sort then it may be best to leave this one out in the first assessment round and have just the straight 'appeal' criteria alone.

Feasibility

This can be as detailed and analysed or as 'top of head' as you have available. Take it from an R&D perspective if it is a new technology or a manufacturing view if it is a new product within existing technology. The power of this approach is that you can mix different levels of understanding; if you are trying to compare a new technology against a variant of an existing one, then this bypasses the means of analysis you might get from your technical team on either and simply asks: 'Is it easy, quite hard or very hard to do?'

Expertise required

This is an alternative for, or adjunct to, feasibility, but often an important one, especially when considering new technologies or categories outside the existing products. For a major multinational, this can often be summarized in three levels:

(a) *In Team* – i.e. expertise readily available
(b) *In Company* – i.e. expertise exists in the company but in another part of the business
(c) *Buy-in* – i.e. to deliver this idea requires expertise from outside the company that would need to be bought in.

Unilever used this approach to good effect in the ice cream business when evaluating new ideas for higher quality ice cream bars. One idea was to use higher quality chocolate rather than the current kind that had been optimized to stick on the ice cream. The technology didn't exist in the ice cream business, but a recent transfer from the yellow fats business immediately saw that the technology with which he was used to working in making margarine would deliver what was required. 'Infeasible' became 'In company' and the idea went on to become Magnum – Unilever's most successful ice cream brand.

Investment

This is another alternative for, or adjunct to, feasibility, that can sometimes be a very decisive element: How much investment is needed to get this idea going? Typically this is about capex. It may be a product that is feasible to manufacture in the existing in-house technology, but would require an entirely new factory to be built to accommodate it. Conversely, it would be an idea where the expertise is external and would require no investment, only a deal with a third party, to begin manufacture. The best bet with this is to keep it very simple: low, medium or high investment.

It can also be used as a marker of marketing investment if you are considering a new brand versus a range extension of an established brand.

Global applicability

How many markets does this idea work in? Again, this is a simple but powerful criterion for selecting ideas. Tune the levels to fit your company needs; it can be made to apply to regions of a country, countries within a continent or continents, depending on your brand's scope. This is especially useful when comparing ideas that appeal strongly to consumers in one geography but not to others, versus an idea that is less appealing but much more widely applicable. This is a tricky one to score so you may have to evolve this to fit your needs. One way to score it is: Local only, A few, Most.

Margin

To be used with care! This is obviously a very important criterion, but one that can easily be misused. It is best to use it where ideas are within well-understood categories with margin structures that can easily be interrogated or compared. In these cases, it becomes critical to guide the team towards ideas that deliver better margins than those currently obtained. Even still, it would be preferable not to weight this too highly as, if an idea is strong, increasing margins is a key brief to the technical and manufacturing teams as well as to the marketing team in terms of pricing.

Passion

The most important criterion of all. How does the team feel about the idea? Do they love it, or is it just another good idea? If you have two ideas, one that fits all your strategic criteria, your brand and the category, but the team feels unmoved by it, and another that is a bit of an oddball, doesn't quite fit all the criteria, but your team simply love it – you must go where the passion is. Ideas with passion behind them will weather many storms and gather smart ideas on their way to launch. Good ideas can easily perish on the rocks of indifference. To paraphrase a Brandgym maxim and apply it to innovation, this one sentence has the power to increase your success rate on its own:

Follow the Passion

A one-sentence innovation masterclass

Table 8.2 presents a fully formed Idea Power matrix, with imaginary scores.

Table 8.2: A fully formed Idea Power Matrix. Which would you choose?.

1 = low 6 = high	Fit to Brand	Consumer Appeal	Relevant Different-iation	Feasibility	Global Applicat-ion	Margin	Passion	Total	Weighted Total
Weighting 1-10	*5*	*9*	*9*	*4*	*4*	*7*	*8*		
Idea 1	6	4	2	3	3	3	2	23	126
Idea 2	3	4	4	3	3	2	4	23	157
Idea 3	3	3	5	2	2	2	6	23	165

Tip: Use even scoring to avoid a 50% score

People will always migrate to a 'safe' score for a new idea if you give them the opportunity. Don't. Have them score each idea between options that have no half-way point, e.g. Terrible, Low, Good, Excellent. That way they are forced to get off the fence.

When to use the Idea Power

There are many points during an innovation process where a rating of this sort can prove useful:

- *During a brainstorming session* – to help to focus effort on where to strengthen weaker ideas.
- *At a review meeting* – to avoid falling back solely on gut instinct and being governed by your mood of the moment. Idea Power is a very good way of avoiding the 'these are *all* crap' moment that can destroy a team's confidence.
- *With a new stakeholder* – when an influential new stakeholder joins a project or suddenly has dominion over it. This kind of rating exercise is an excellent way to bring their point of view in without bringing the project (and ideas) to a shuddering halt.

- *After Consumer Research Debrief* – to avoid the consumer view dominating all others. It is useful to whip out your matrix and get the scores up on the wall. It puts things in perspective and helps to focus the effort where it is needed to improve ideas with the new insight.

Benefits of using Idea Power

Evaluating ideas at any stage in their gestation is a tricky business, fraught with egos, politics, poor past experiences and unwieldy methodologies. Defining and agreeing a set of simple criteria and getting colleagues to score ideas against them removes a lot of the subjectivity and allows everyone the benefit of the same objectivity – which is the right frame of mind for effective evaluation. Beyond this there are other practical benefits of using Idea Power for evaluation:

- *Scenario modelling*: Having all ideas set in a matrix and scored, allows you to play with the scoring and the weighting of each criterion to see what happens given certain different scenarios. For instance, you could see what happens if you bought company *x*, or if a competitor launched into the market, or even if certain events happened in society that were beyond your control. All can be discussed, modelled and accounted for.
- *Traceability*: If matrices are used consistently throughout your process and stored, then you can trace the decisions that were made and why. This is perfect if you want to review a project (or get audited). It is a tremendously useful tool for recording ideas and thus making sure none is lost.
- *Involving others*: Many people want to stick their oar into innovation projects and give you the benefit of their experience. This can be useful or extremely destructive. Without understanding the context for an idea or set of ideas, someone with a different perspective can push your project in a totally new or negative direction. It is not wrong to get fresh perspectives, they can be just the tonic you need, but they need to be brought in with care; using Idea Power allows people free reign to share their views and lay out their evaluation clearly so that each point can be debated and the misunderstanding be separated from the flashes of important insight.

   This tool permits a very wide variety of inputs to be usefully captured and recorded: chairman, suppliers, other teams or roving experts – all can add their views helpfully.
- *Focus*: One of the central benefits of using this tool is that it assists in focusing your attention down onto the key issue. By flexing the scoring or weighting you can see very quickly which aspect of an idea is either its Achilles' heel or its core strength. This is very useful for propelling teams along the right path when developing ideas into winning propositions.

Building winning ideas

Boiling ideas down from many to a few shouldn't be difficult. The critical thing is not to spend too much time and resource doing it. By quickly coming to a conclusion on which ideas to pursue you give your team two important benefits:

- more time
- a chance to go round again.

Using quantitative concept testing

By doing a concept test and inputting the scores as the consumer Appeal in an Idea Power evaluation you can get the benefit of more accurate input from quantitative testing as well as a more rounded view that incorporates internal issues such as feasibility. Ideas will no longer be killed off just because they scored poorly on a concept test. If they still have loads of team passion behind them and they fit the brand vision beautifully, you can decide to go round again and improve the concept. That is the important objectivity the use of an Idea Power evaluation can give you.

Key takeouts

- Bringing ideas to life through early prototyping and visualization is vital to help people see their true potential.
- Performing ideas rather than presenting them gives the best platform for evaluation.
- A good balance of objective evaluation (including quantitative concept testing) and experience based gut instinct makes for the best prioritization.
- Using an Idea Power Matrix can help to remove politics and summarize the most accurate evaluation from many people.
- Prioritizing innovation ideas need not take months; it can be done effectively very quickly.

Checklist: Nozzle

	Yes	No
1 Do you always feel you have chosen the best ideas?	☐	☐
2 Do you perform ideas using props, examples, mock-ups, etc?	☐	☐

3 Do you take into account all views but still get to a clear decision?

☐   ☐

4 Do you take decisions quickly on which ideas to progress?

☐   ☐

5 Is choosing the best ideas fun?

☐   ☐

6 Do you keep and recycle ideas even though they scored badly in concept testing?

☐   ☐

 Handover

Now you have quickly and effectively got down to the one or two ideas with real potential and saved yourself huge chunks of time and money in the process (and had some fun), it's time to spend that extra time and money in building the ideas into launchable winners. The next chapter deals with turning good ideas into winning mixes without getting mired by the compromises of 'how it's done today'.

Rocketing: Expander

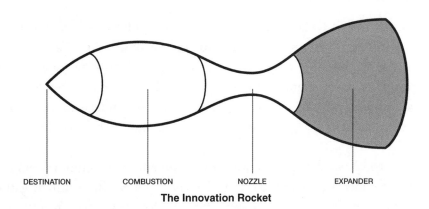

CHAPTER 9

DESTINATION   COMBUSTION   NOZZLE   EXPANDER

The Innovation Rocket

 Headlines

Execution is the only innovation consumers ever see. If a key part of your idea does not end up on shelf, then it might as well never have existed. To get ideas through the mix development minefield you need a positive attitude throughout the business, so that everyone is adding value and not just spotting flaws. Make sure your idea is singing through all 360 degrees of the mix. Then in the final stage of evaluation, put your innovation into a real test market, not a simulated one, to get real feedback. Your innovation work is not over at launch. Watching and making tweaks over the first year is a critical step for long-term success.

Keeping positive

The Expander is the fourth phase of the Innovation Rocket; this is where the one or two chosen ideas emerging from the Nozzle are built into launch ready mixes. It seems that the usual way for this part of the development process to take place is chipping corners off ideas and beating them into a standardized shape to make them fit in. This means, as the idea originator, your role becomes more about saving what you can from the original notion as it goes through the marketing machine than about anything more positive. The focus of the Expander process is to counter the inexorable forces of standardization and add as much value as possible across all facets of the marketing mix. This means that when the day arrives for consumers to see and hear it, it delivers the maximum possible impact – i.e. it gets tried, bought again and earns a place on the weekly shopping list.

Innovation Antibodies

The chief issue that needs to be faced in this part of the idea development process is that your business naturally rejects good ideas. Not on purpose, but as a matter of course. Why? Because they represent change, and change is inefficient. Change goes against what 90% of the people in your organization are trying to do every day. Therefore, to innovate successfully you need to push hard, very hard. Hard enough, in fact, to move all the people implicated in your business along with you. This is what makes the final development phase so difficult.

There you are, you have changed the way your team approaches innovation, built a clear vision for your new idea, generated loads of high quality ideas from insight garnered from farther a field than ever before, quickly and efficiently focused down onto those ideas that ignite passion and show real potential, and had a significant development budget signed off after your performance at the board meeting won you an innovation Oscar. Now you face your toughest challenge – getting your idea turned from a mock-up and a written concept into a fully fledged manufactured product surrounded by a full and funky marketing mix. This is when you encounter the innovation antibodies: those parts of the organization that seek out change and try to neutralize it, rather like a good air freshener. The same people who have eliminated waste, removed unnecessary duplication and built your company into an engine of profit, will see only the inefficiencies, extra investment and hassle that a new innovation will bring.

'We've just aligned all our buying procedures and channel management strategies across the whole business – it's taken two years, now you want to change it!'

Maybe it's sourcing organic ingredients for the first time, addressing a new buying point at your big customers, or maybe just changing packaging materials. Whatever it is – what seemed like a simple bit of added value for consumers becomes the cause for raised eyebrows, exasperated looks and shaking heads up and down the supply chain. And can you blame them? They are just doing their jobs.

Even at 3M, that doyen if the innovation world, innovations have to fight hard and long to see the light of day. One of the presentations at a recent marketing conference was from a chap at 3M. We are all familiar with this kind of conference: a series of topics with grand strategic titles like 'Seeking out and Constructing Optimum Brand Value in High

Competition Marketspaces' that are actually just a random assembly of presentations from whoever the conference organizers could muster at the last minute. This presenter started with a picture of his daughter and then went on to tell us about his job. One of his claims to fame was that he proudly told us that he had shut down the Post-it project. He had told Art Fry, the Post-It inventor, that there was no more money, no more resource and no more patience left for his not-very-sticky-little-pieces-of-yellow-paper. He ordered Fry to stop what he was doing immediately and get on with something more worth-while. He didn't do this just once, but three times. In all, he told us, executives at 3M shut down the Post-It development project five times, or possibly more, he wasn't sure. Of course the project did carry on and the result is a multi-billion dollar success story. So, in reality, the corporate gene that makes 3M such a relentlessly successful innovator is not just its ability to come up with good ideas, but its ability to accept people breaking the rules. Interesting. If someone at your company does the equivalent of sticking their fingers in their ears and singing 'la-la-la' when a senior executive tells them to cease and desist a project – what would happen? To be a great innovator, maybe the answer should be 'they get tolerated' rather than 'they get toasted'.

What is needed is a **mindset change** when concepts are being developed into launchable products: to change from a focus of evaluating ideas to one of expanding ideas as they move towards launch. This mindset change needs to stop your company's powerful innovation antibodies from attacking new ideas. Instead it needs to foster an instinct to continually strengthen ideas so that they are tougher and fitter for their first step into the harsh outside world.

Expand not evaluate

The principle is simple: if you spend more time and effort during development in building a new concept than in evaluating it, you will end up with a stronger offer at launch. Dazzlingly straightforward as this principle may be, it does not appear to be the one that drives allocation of resources during development at most multinationals. If a business has, say, 100 units of resource to spend on developing an identified priority concept through to launch, how should it be spent? It is of course sensible to allocate some of the resource in getting an objective evaluation so that you can see where you are. But to spend 75 of the 100 units, or even more, on evaluation, testing, market potential estimation, benchmarking, etc., seems unwise at best, and downright stupid at worst. But this seems to be the way that things are going. Our accountants' desire for measurement and accountability is driving us all to evaluate far more than we expand.

This is not going to generate better innovations.

We need to add value, strengthen, build and improve our chosen ideas more than we evaluate, compare, pick apart, and check them.

There are four key aspects to this:

- Be a builder not a knocker
- Execution is everything
- Get real feedback
- Launch then tweak

Be a builder not a knocker

I have no particular bone to pick with wrecking ball operators, I'm sure it's a profitable business, but I bet they don't get as much credit as the construction guys. When new buildings like the Gherkin in London go up and everyone stands agog at its architectural mastery, it is not to the guys who tore down whatever was there before that everyone raises their metaphorical glasses. It's to the builders and architects. In marketing, as in life, it pays to be a constructor not a demolisher.

A few techniques are outlined here, with examples, of how to bring this mindset into your everyday marketing work. This is not something that requires a week-long training session to bring out your inner positivity, but a practical set of techniques that you can use immediately to good effect.

Combine ideas

The first step is simple; don't just choose between ideas – combine them. There is value in all ideas, however stupid they may appear at first glance. Find the good bits and build them in, rather than discard the whole thing out of hand. In a project this means regularly going back over the ideas you have generated and seeing what can be used to add to your core concept. There may have been some little notion that on its own was worthless, but when tagged onto a big idea, adds real value.

Flower power

There is one aspect of the reinvented VW Beetle that has always caught the eye: the little plastic vase on the dashboard (Figure 9.1). You never see a Beetle without a flower in this vase. This 1 euro piece of plastic is the difference between it being an ordinary

BE/0016

Figure 9.1: VW Beetle dashboard vase.

VW-Golf-with-a-different-body-shape and the reincarnation of 60's flower power that has caught the imagination of a new generation. It may be that, early on in the innovation project to rebirth the famous Beetle, someone threw in the idea of making a 'flower power car'. This clearly was a no-go for the German car maker as the core concept, but it was not discarded. Somewhere along the line in the development process this little idea was picked up again, nurtured and combined into the 100% modern car in a simple practical way. It helps to turn it into a fresh version of the original, rather than just a retro retread.

Get a positive attitude

At Procter & Gamble they have an enviable reputation for successful innovation and are currently delivering above average profits in nearly all areas of their business. This has a lot to do with their attitude to innovation. In their business they see a positive attitude to innovation and creativity as a core business competence. Craig Wynett, general manager of future growth initiatives at P&G stated in the *Harvard Business Review*'s 'Inspiring Innovation' series in 2002 that 'What we've done to encourage innovation is make it ordinary'. His explanation reveals an insistence on a positive attitude to new ideas:

By that I mean we don't separate it from the rest of our business. Many companies make innovation front page news, and all that special attention has a paradoxical effect. By serving it up as something exotic, you isolate it from what's normal... At P&G, we think of creativity not as a mysterious gift of the talented few but as the everyday task of making non-obvious connections – bringing together things that don't normally go together... Isolating innovation from mainstream business can produce a dangerous cultural side-effect: Creativity and leadership can be perceived as opposites. This artificial disconnect means that innovators often lack the visibility and clout to compete for the resources necessary for success.

A positive accident

Back to 3M again. They are always good for an innovation anecdote, and the invention of Scotchguard, the fabric protector, is no exception. A 3M researcher was experimenting with fluorochemical polymers one day when she accidentally spilled some of the solution on her tennis shoes. She tried to clean it off but couldn't. She tried soap and water, alcohol and a whole host of solvents but nothing worked. Rather than leave it at that, her training to look for new ideas kicked in and she realized that if she had a substance that was so resistant to solvents, maybe it could be used to protect textiles from solvents. Further development of this idea proved her right and a major new product line was born. Her positive attitude turned spilled polymer into spectacular profits.

So how can you imbue a more consistently positive attitude into your team – particularly those who come into the idea development process from outside the core innovation team? A simple technique can help enormously...

BE NICE

This is not as simplistic as it sounds. Whenever you are in an innovation situation, a concept review, brainstorm or any meeting where you are sharing ideas of any sort, you must have a **strict behaviour code** of being nice. This means that any reaction or comment on an idea must be couched in one of two ways, and two ways only:

> *What I like about this idea...*
> *How to overcome issue X...*

This is very powerful and works surprisingly well. It focuses the conversation on the positive things and not on why something does not work or fit. The issues or problems are automatically surfaced as requests for solutions, rather than barriers that tend to bring

Box 9.1: The Innovation Antibody Review	
MD:	Simpkins, let's have a look at these concepts you are developing
Simpkins:	Right away. This one is the Foot Long. . .
MD:	Kids can't eat that much
Simpkins:	No, er. . .I suppose they can't [puts idea aside]. This one is our Fresh concept – moving into the more premium end of the market
MD:	Have you seen how much a chill chain costs?
Simpkins:	Well, no. We hadn't got that far in. . .er. . .[puts idea aside] How about this one?
MD:	What is it?
Simpkins:	Orange flavour.
MD:	Well, orange flavour is cheap to source.
Simpkins:	Yes. . .and popular.
MD:	Right.
	[pause]
	Back to the drawing board, Simpkins.
Simpkins:	I'll get right onto it.

everything to a grinding halt. A typical conversation might go something like the one in Box 9.1. In this example all ideas are rejected and our trusty marketing manager goes back to his project with an empty concept folder and depleted confidence. Now, what happens if we imbue our trusty team with a positive attitude and invoke the strict 'be nice' rule? See Box 9.2 for a rerun of the conversation.

A wholly different experience! What was a slow grind to a halt resulting in a dejected team member leaving the room to start over, has now become a useful building of ideas resulting in an energized team member leaving the room with confidence to strengthen his concepts.

The example may be a bit simplistic but it really works in practice. Try it in your next innovation meeting. Put a sign on the door that dictates an Innovation Code to be obeyed by all. You could try photocopying the one in Box 9.3.

Senior Service

This is particularly important when bringing in senior executives to cast their eye over a concept in development. If we take our usual routine of just presenting something to them and then standing back, they will most probably immediately point out 10 ways your idea

---

Box 9.2: The Positive Attitude Review

MD:	Simpkins, let's have a look at these concepts you are developing
Simpkins:	Right away. This one is the Foot Long...
MD:	How can we get kids to eat that much?
Simpkins:	Maybe cut it into 3 portions, or target it at teenagers? This one is our Fresh concept – moving into the more premium end of the market
MD:	How can we get around the high chill chain costs?
Simpkins:	We could see how much of a premium people are willing to pay for fresh. How about this one sir?
MD:	What is it?
Simpkins:	Orange flavour.
MD:	I like orange flavour, and it's cheap to source, but how can we differentiate it?
Simpkins:	We could do Mandarin, Orange & Mango or maybe explore other citrus flavours?
MD:	Right.
	[pause]
	Let's have another conversation when you've developed them on a bit, Simpkins. Good work.
Simpkins:	Thanks.

Box 9.3: The Innovation Code

Be Nice

When reacting to an idea, say:

- What I like...
- How to overcome...

---

will fail/won't be profitable/is just plain wrong. As stated in Chapter 4, this kind of input can kill energy, ideas and sometime careers. Taking the 'Be Nice' innovation code a step further, I suggest you make a point of getting senior input focused on solving problems and/or adding ideas. Do this by introducing your idea differently; try presenting the problems you are experiencing and asking for solutions.

Getting senior executives to Be Nice to new ideas

Before...

You: What do you think of our new youth targeted idea?

Senior: We've targeted teens before and it was a complete disaster. . . . We're not Nike you know. . . . We haven't got the budget to get Beckham in our ads. . .etc.

After...

You: This is the new youth targeted idea we are developing, we just can't seem to find a packaging solution that will meet our cost target and be cool for teens.

Senior: Have you spoken to Henri at our French operation? He is working on some new low-cost shrink wrapping that might help. . .

In one sentence, instead of telling you why your idea doesn't appeal to him, the senior executive has imparted unique knowledge that could be the making of your idea. Alternatively, you could play it even more openly, and still avoid stimulating the innovation antibodies. . .

Getting senior executives to Be Nice to new ideas . . . again

You: This is the new youth targeted idea we are developing and we are challenging ourselves on how to double its potential. Do you have any ideas or thoughts from your experience on that?

Senior: How about going to Guatemala? The new general manager there is very keen on new products, you can do launches cheaper than in our core markets and you'll learn as you go . . .

Again, in one sentence a whole new avenue of input has arisen that was not in your original scope. And, what is more, you have flattered the senior executive – always a good thing!

Use research to build not destroy

I love research. Love it. I can't do an innovation project without talking to consumers in some form or another. I also hate research. I hate it with a passion and a loathing. Especially during the later stages of an innovation project. Am I mad? Bipolar? No – just very aware that research gets badly misused in this part of the innovation journey. Once you have reached the part where there is only one idea left – research most likely having been used to kill off the other ideas in a quasi-Darwinian survival of the fittest bloodbath – research gets tougher still. The tests get bigger, uglier and much more serious; econometric modelling of likely sales uplift, share gain and other secondary and tertiary calculations get loaded onto the shoulders of what is still a single paragraph of text with accompanying imagery. Yikes! And what will be the next thing that accountants will believe we can forecast by sophisticated modelling: share price? This would be as close to insanity as marketers could get (bar that moment when we convince ourselves that our 2-for-1 offer is actually 'strategic').

Yes, it's important to find out how motivating your new idea is versus the current offer. But sitting back and letting the bald numbers do the talking is not going to get you the optimum result. It's too dangerous.

All washed up

Consider what happened to an innovation project in a global detergent brand at just this stage. It was a multi-region project, all where banking on it delivering something really significant for their next year plans. R&D had come up with some clever technology that showed real promise for delivering consumer relevant cleaning benefits. The team were fighting tight deadlines, strict cost targets and stiff competition both from the low-cost players and the premium brands. This was a tough project, not least because of the immense complexity of innovating for 40+ markets in multiple formats, sizes and mix combinations. They needed every bit of luck going.

Then they did their first quant concept test. The results were not bad, but they were not good either; they exceeded the benchmark for the category but lost out against the existing offer by 3% on top two box scores. What happened when the results were presented?

- A wave of disappointment washed instantly over the whole team.
- R&D jumped on the defensive and started reneging on their claims 'We never said it could actually do that . . . '
- The regions, until now held in unison by a common objective, instantly started infighting; out came their 'plan B' concepts and conversations of 'I never thought it would work anyway . . . ' along with 'we don't think this is a concept for our region. . .'.
- Someone suggested that they quit the whole project right now, as it was 'dead'.
- Senior confidence drained from the project like beer from a rugby player's glass.
- The next few weeks were spent in endless justification and back-pedalling discussions with all and sundry.
- The project was continued, but after a month's hiatus. It now had an additional, tougher quantitative test, crow-barred in later that quarter, pushing the timelines into the following year, missing the window for two of the big regions.

The team then had to get back to work – turning the new idea into a maximum impact launch – with minimal business confidence, an increased admin/testing burden and colleagues who were all now looking to their next (more advantageous) assignment. And all because some 1000 randomly selected people thought that this particular paragraph of text with a standard stock-book picture was 3% less interesting than the product they have been buying, using and trusting for the last 5–50 years.

Keep Building

The innovation antibodies in this company where particularly virulent, but in my view there is a better way to deal with such a situation. Rather than jumping to the negative when bad research results loom, you should think to yourself 'what can we do to improve the concept?' 'How can we make it more impactful/relevant/differentiated?' In short you should be using research studies to learn and build rather than test and destroy.

Better to ask 'what can we learn' than 'how did it do?'.

The problem, as in our detergent example, is that research can end up driving the whole innovation process. It becomes the focus of the project. All eyes are only on how your concept scores, not on whether it's a good idea or not. Added to this is the practical fact that research is a big ticket item and takes up a lot of time and resource. It is therefore only too easy to let it take over and become the centrepiece of the whole project. It is vital that we put the idea at the centre of the project. All other parts of the process are there to build and maximize the idea. Figure 9.2 shows the difference between projects where research has taken over as the driver, against the idea remaining as the driving force.

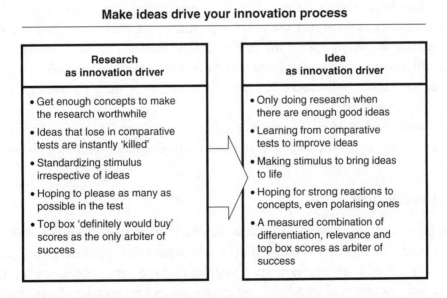

Make ideas drive your innovation process

Research as innovation driver	Idea as innovation driver
• Get enough concepts to make the research worthwhile	• Only doing research when there are enough good ideas
• Ideas that lose in comparative tests are instantly 'killed'	• Learning from comparative tests to improve ideas
• Standardizing stimulus irrespective of ideas	• Making stimulus to bring ideas to life
• Hoping to please as many as possible in the test	• Hoping for strong reactions to concepts, even polarising ones
• Top box 'definitely would buy' scores as the only arbiter of success	• A measured combination of differentiation, relevance and top box scores as arbiter of success

Figure 9.2: Ideas vs Research as innovation process driver.

Execution is everything

Knob Twiddling

Lyndsay Owen Jones is the charismatic and hugely successful head of L'Oréal. It is the company that has changed the face of cosmetics and has grown consistently through innovation – very successful innovation in one of the most competitive marketplaces. Every innovation that is planned to be launched is presented to the CEO. That in itself is a clear signal of how seriously they take new ideas. As he only wants to see prototypes presented, not PowerPoint, a tremendous amount of time and energy is devoted to the minutiae of execution. When the fruit-based Garnier shampoo Fructis was being prepared for launch the team spent months tweaking and retweaking the little knobbly top on the lid. This small packaging component is a symbol of the brand's difference. L'Oréal saw this as a critical piece of the launch equation. Judging by its subsequent success they were clearly not wrong. L'Oréal's attention to detail across 360° of execution is one of their key success factors as a world leading innovator.

Use the full 360°

When consumers meet your idea for the first time, it is very seldom, if ever, the way you imagine. They are not clear minded and open and relaxed, ready to consider your idea and compare its benefits to the rest of the offers in a logical calm way. They most probably see half an advert as they channel surf, use the new product at a friend's house without noticing, and then see it on the wrong part of the shelf where the shelf-stacker has managed to squeeze it in. What this means is that you had better make sure that your new idea is singing out from every angle, every touch point and every part of the mix with one clear message. Otherwise it might just go unnoticed.

Think through every part of the mix when developing a new concept. A handy checklist is laid out in Table 9.1 for you to review in concept development sessions with your team.

Get real feedback

One piece of research that is being built onto the end of many standard innovation processes is the Simulated Test Market, or STM. This is where your new product, in full packaging, is presented to a nationally representative sample of consumers, sometimes on a realistic retail shelf, and accompanied by advertising or sometimes 'stealomatic' advertising that uses existing ads cobbled together into a new script. The subsequent probably/definitely would

Table 9.1: 360° Mix checklist.

Element	Challenge	Action
Product Benefit	• Is your new benefit consumer perceivable? • Are you different enough from competitors? • What is new/emerging – are you leading?	

Product Format	• Are you unique enough across:
	  – Shape
	  – Smell
	  – Colour
	  – Texture
	  – In use characteristics (e.g. pouring)
	• Portion size: how can you be more relevant?	

Pack Design	• How can you stand out. . .
	  – vs. competitors
	  – Across markets
	  – With best in class	

Consumer Communications	• Who's cutting through? How can you? • Are you getting the most you can out of new media? • What media assets can you create?	
Intermediary/ Professional Communications	• How can you be recommended more? • What value can you bring to intermediaries' lives/jobs? • What other brands have relationships you could piggyback?	
In-Store	• What are the retailer's objectives – can you work with them? • Are you considering secondary siting? • Who is cutting through in store? What can you learn/steal? • How can your secondary packaging bring a benefit to the retailer or consumer?	
New Channels	• What other channels are your competitors in? • What new channels are emerging? • What new channels could you create?	
Pack Structure	• How can you add a benefit with the pack? • Are you unique enough in shape and substrate? • How can you improve your closure? • How can you improve home storage? • What about disposability, recycling?	
Pricing	• Are new approaches being used? • What can you steal from other categories (e.g. Mobile phones)?	

buy scores (and the answers to various other nattily worded questions) are dropped into a complex algorithm and crunched by laptopped pointy-headed analysts to mimic what would happen in real life. Media weights are modelled and consumer responses are mapped onto standard mean scores across a dizzying array of categories. The result comes out as a number with a dollar sign attached. That's when businesses start taking notice. This test models the sales you would expect if you launched your new product. Caps off to the smart research businesses for delivering what the accountants have always wanted – a way round the creative bit in marketing to get straight to the bottom line. Surely this is it; innovation Nirvana, where you can measure the likely return of an idea?

Not quite.

There are many caveats with research studies, but none more so that with STMs. If you multiply the uncertainty level of each of the assumptions along the way you get to a large number, large enough to make the accuracy of the answer seriously questionable. Is it precise? Undoubtedly so, from the mathematical perspective. Is it accurate? A large pinch of salt please. It gives you an indication of your idea's likely performance, which is good. But it's VERY expensive and takes a LONG time.

Real test markets

How about doing an RTM instead? You know, a Real Test Market. Where real consumers get to see real ads, buy real products in a real store and give you real feedback on your idea's potential through real sales data. This involves launching with a limited distribution and watching what happens. Many businesses do this simply because they cannot afford to do the simulated version. Big businesses who do have multi-million dollar research budgets should take a lead from their smaller cousins and get their feet wet earlier with their new ideas.

A breeze

Bacardi took this approach with their phenomenally successful innovation – Bacardi Breezer. When they developed it (a copy of what was happening in one part of the US) they were not sure how well it would work in the UK, so they targeted a small region in the north and waited. When the bar owners couldn't get enough of it to satisfy their thirsty female clientele, Bacardi upped production and went for a larger launch. This led to some major listings and then 'the deluge', as the then marketing manager termed it. In no time it was selling several times more volume than anything else in their portfolio. On reflection, the team put down a great deal of this success to the slow burn nature of the launch. They were able to see the kind of outlets in which it sold best, to whom and thus where to target their salesforce. It also gave them tremendous confidence when striking the big deals with the major grocers and bar chains – real sales per outlet data beats any simulated test analysis when talking to buyers.

The chief drawback of this approach, oft cited by cautious multinationals, is the fallout for the brand if a new idea doesn't work. 'Consumers will lose confidence in my brand.' This is a perfectly sensible concern, but it is overstated. Much like when considering pack design changes – consumer are in most cases much more ready to accept new designs than the brand team think they are – marketers fear failure much more than they should. Actually, a bit of failure is quite healthy for a brand. Most big brands are dealing with failures all the time, they just don't view them that way; bad ads, poor flavour variants and the like just get left behind along the path. Consumers barely notice them as long as the core offer stays healthy. So when approaching new innovation, a healthy perspective on likely failure is the right approach. It all depends on your viewpoint.

Google it

Google are a company that share this perspective: Marissa Meyer, director of consumer Web products, is a highly influential cog in Google's innovation machinery. She decides what is ready to be put in front of the two founders at their regular innovation meetings. They then decide to take an idea into full launch or send it back for more tinkering. What Mayer thinks will be essential for continued innovation is for Google to keep its sense of fearlessness. 'I like to launch [products] early and often. That has become my mantra,' she says. She mentions Apple Computer and Madonna. 'Nobody remembers the Newton or the Sex book. Consumers remember your average over time. That philosophy frees you from fear.'

A bit of an animal

As a good example of a major multinational doing real tests instead of simulated tests, let's look at the brand Peperami (Figure 9.3). Unilever Foods was looking for some quick wins in the UK and this brand was a local jewel that had not been invested in for a few years. A meat snack with a great personality, Peperami had been a strong success in the tough UK snacking market but it now languished unloved, its growth stalled. The team, however, believed there was profitable growth to be had through some innovation.

Did they start a project and follow the full funnel process? Was that the best way to ensure success?

No.

Figure 9.3: Peperami – "A bit of an animal".

The team created a myriad of ideas, working up those they felt passionate about into lifelike mixes with their design agency Core Design, then choosing the five most likely, based on their experience and intuition. They did no formal consumer research, only a couple of consumer groups in their in-house facility. They didn't do concept tests, design research or simulated test markets. They went with their hunches and launched four of the five (Figure 9.4). The whole process from start to launch took five months.

After three months the team took stock and decided to focus all their energy and above the line support on Firestick, which was a significant success. Sarni they left as it was selling relatively well, but Dunkers and Canniballs they took off the market. Enough growth and profit was generated to justify this approach.

Figure 9.4: Peperami innovations in the UK.

Table 9.2: Rocketing vs Funneling: the costs (author's estimates).

	Rocketing	Funneling
Process	Develop 5 ideas, no research, just design & launch	Full Funnel research process
Development cost	Approx. £250k	Approx. £1m
Time to launch	5 months	12–18 months

This was a fast, Rocketing-style innovation process. But would it have been just as successful if they had followed the formal funnel process and whittled their ideas down to one through rounds of qualitative and quantitative research? This lays out some interesting questions: What would the difference between the two approaches have been in terms of:

- total development cost?
- time to launch?

Estimates from the team involved are presented in Table 9.2.

The team's Rocketing-style innovation approach led to a launch 7–12 months earlier at a quarter of the cost of the formal funnel process. What seemed at first glance to be a wanton waste of precious resource, turns out to have been a shrewd and cost-effective innovation method.

> ### Peperami summary
>
> - Spend more on development than evaluation
> - Launch multiple ideas fast
> - Let the winners sell themselves

The success virus

In a multinational business where global brands operate across many countries, another way of getting real consumer feedback is by taking a lead market approach to innovation. More than just leading an innovation project on behalf of the globe, this is about local countries developing and launching their own innovations, within the parameters of a clearly defined global brand, and then the rest of the world rolling the good ones out. If a company is structured to manage quick roll-outs without re-doing the testing in each market, then this is a fast way of doing global innovation.

Hero, the Swiss jam and fruit drinks company, launched its successful Fruit2Day fruit shots in this way. It was a big success in Holland first and was then rolled out to other markets. Likewise Wella, the hair care brand, first developed and launched its Studioline range in Switzerland, then rolled this out to other markets where it has been a significant success for them.

This approach is like a 'success virus' as the buzz of one market's success speeds up the adoption of the idea in other markets, keen to capture the new growth as soon as they can. The clear obstacle to this approach is the 'not invented here' syndrome that is sadly still prevalent in many businesses. This is very effective antivirus software and in the wrong company will turn this fast, lower budget innovation approach into a large, slow-moving and ineffective way to grow ideas globally. This is dealt with in Chapter 13, 'How to avoid the pitfalls'.

Launch then tweak

Too often marketers labour and labour to get to the perfect mix – one that can't be faulted by anyone or any test that the organization can throw at it. Then and only then is it deemed fit to launch. This is a fallacy we need to get rid of. The one test that will surely show up some cracks in the veneer of perfection that we have lovingly polished onto our idea is to *launch* it. Competitors and retailers (in particular) have a way of behaving not quite the way we had imagined. It's as if they have minds of their own. It's too easy to get to launch and then stand back hoping to admire the view and spend most of your time counting the cash and garnering the accolades. Instead, it should be the time to continue the hard work. Astronauts know this well. The launch may be the most perilous and thrilling moment of your journey, but it is not the be all and end all. Many hours of skilful piloting and twiddling knobs (a technical term) is needed before the destination is reached and the final orbit is established.

Their days were numbered

Having spent billions on a brand new licence, Hutchinson Telecom entered the burgeoning UK mobile phone market with a bold new brand '3'. It was launched with great fanfare as the vanguard of hi-tech 3G services. They were the first to go to market with new 'added value' services and although their network was limited to major cities, they believed what the whole industry wanted to believe; that consumers would fall over themselves to get infotainment. What quickly became apparent was that consumers couldn't see the benefit of these limited services versus all the other entertainment and information outlets they had available. Frankly, they couldn't care less about 3G (and to date, despite many billions spent, people still don't). '3' saw this very quickly in the slow take-up of their phones. They realized they had to alter their offer drastically and quickly. So they changed tack. From being the harbinger of a new age of mobile connectivity they became the 'loads of free minutes' cheap calls people. This 'launch and tweak' approach saved their business, their brand and their butts. Now, several years down the track, they are venturing back into added value services by bolstering their core cheap calls offer with added entertainment – music and music videos. This is as a means of differentiating themselves from the hoards of other cheap calls offers on the market.

'3' summary

- Believed strongly in their idea and went for it
- Accepted that they were wrong and rang the alarm bells early
- Changed their offer quickly to work in the market

Key Takeouts

1 Your whole development team needs a positive attitude of expanding ideas not evaluating them to get through the development minefield.
2 Focus senior managers on building ideas and solving problems not just spotting flaws.
3 Make sure the ideas are driving your innovation process, not the research.
4 Develop ideas into 360° mixes as early as possible to increase your chances of success.
5 Do real test markets rather than simulated ones.
6 Don't be tempted to launch and leave a new innovation; real success needs a launch and tweak approach.
7 What is executed is the only innovation that consumers see.

Checklist: Combustion

	YES	NO
1 Do your ideas always emerge at launch stronger and more distinct rather than weaker and less distinct?	☐	☐
2 Do you build ideas into 360° mixes early in the development process?	☐	☐
3 Do senior managers build ideas and solve problems, not just spot flaws?	☐	☐

4 Do you rely on real test markets, not simulated ones?   ☐   ☐

5 Are you keeping a close eye on launched innovations and   ☐   ☐
   tweaking the mix to perfect it?

 ## Handover

Congratulations! You've reached the end of the Innovation Rocket process. We've been through all four stages: Destination, Combustion, Nozzle and Expander. Feel free to jump for joy now that you have the tools to turn every innovation project from a slow slide down a funnel full of rusty admin nails, into a rocket ride rammed with great ideas. So who does this well already? The next chapter gives you 10 examples of people who make it look really easy.

The Entertainment

PART IV

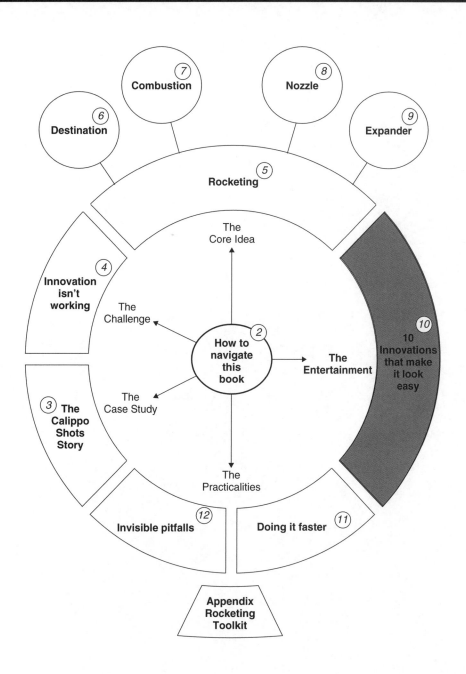

Ten innovations that make it look easy

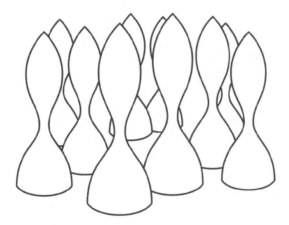

CHAPTER 10

Innovation shortcuts

So who is turning innovation into rocket science out there? Here are 10 brands that have taken on the most difficult challenge and succeeded. They have set out to create growth in their core markets through the strength and execution of new ideas within their brands and won. Of course, all great marketing looks obvious in hindsight. It's easy to say "Well they would do that wouldn't they?" when you see a truly great innovation, but it's another story when you are faced with the seemingly impossible task of creating growth in your own core market. As inspiration when you are next brainstorming, each one of these has been summarized as an innovation shortcut.

The chapter is intended as a bit of a break for those who have made it this far in the book. You have read through the core thesis on Rocketing and now you can put your mental feet up and leaf through some easily digestible sound bites on brands you will know. They are written in a one-to-a-page format so that, should the inspiration strike you, you could photocopy them and use them elsewhere as innovation case studies.

New brands are innovations too

Two new brands have also been added to this list; both Gü, the scrummy chocolate desserts, and Ocado, the UK online grocery retailer, launched into commoditized and very tough retailer own-brand-dominated categories, and both came out on top through the strength of their ideas.

As they have innovated their categories, they have been dragged into this chapter.

The 10 Innovations

Brand	Innovation	Shortcut
Danone	Actimel	Create a new daily habit
T-Mobile	Mates Rates	Sell the benefit not the feature
Hovis	Best of Both	Resolve a fundamental trade-off
Motorola	RAZR	Never underestimate the power of design
American Express	Red	When everyone else zigs, zag
Renault	Scenic	Break category rules
Johnson's	Holiday Skin™	Create hybrids to build new categories
Yoplait Petits Filous	Frubes	Deliver extraordinary convenience

New brand ideas in commoditized super-tough categories:

Brand	Innovation	Shortcut
Gü	Desserts	Premiumize a commoditized category
Ocado	Online Grocery	Add service in a commodity market

Figure 10.1: Danone Actimel.

Shortcut:	Create a new daily habit

Innovation: **Danone Actimel**

Tough challenge	Copy the market leader (Yakult) but make it differentiated and ownable. Make it more accessible and mainstream, and deliver a strong functional benefit with credibility from your brand for the first time.
Winning proposition	• The (genuinely) delicious everyday mini yoghurt drink with friendly bacteria that restore your natural defences.
Why it is better	• Managed to deliver a genuinely delicious taste together with an accessible but credible level of functional benefit – 'friendly bacteria'.
Why it is brand building	• Delivers perfectly on the core Danone equities of tasty, healthy, dairy goodness. • Adds real functional health credentials to the brand that they are now exploiting elsewhere.
How it builds business	• Does not cannibalize other Danone offers. • Creates a daily habit that drives huge volumes. • Creates a new category in which they dominate.
See also:	Baby Bel.

Figure 10.2: T-Mobile Mates Rates.

Shortcut:	Sell the benefit not the feature

Innovation: **T-Mobile Mates Rates**

Tough challenge   To create differentiation and preference in a price led commodity category.

Winning proposition
- Cheaper calls among your friends on the same network.

Why it is better
- Creative packaging and pinpoint targeting of an existing idea.
- Selling the benefit (more fun with your mates) not the feature (on-net low cost calls).

Why it is brand building
- Successfully targets a youthful cohort with a totally relevant offer, bringing youth and insight into a bland brand.

How it builds business
- Enables and encourages people to adopt one network provider among their mates to get cheaper calls.
- Drives share and loyalty (a network provider's dream!).

See also: Vodafone Stop The Clock.

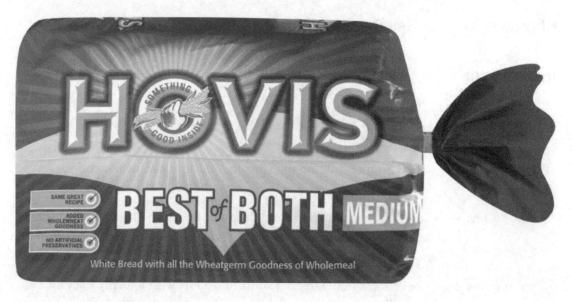

Figure 10.3: Hovis Best of Both.

Shortcut:	Resolve a fundamental trade-off

Innovation: **Hovis Best of Both**

Tough challenge   To create relevant differentiation in a commoditized category.

Winning proposition
- White bread with all the wheat germ goodness of wholemeal.

Why it is better
- Breaks a fundamental trade-off mums have been making for decades; the kids prefer white, but brown bread is healthier.

Why it is brand building
- Delivers on the core brand offer of natural goodness with a totally relevant new benefit for families and a Unique Selling Point for Hovis.

How it builds business
- Brings new and lapsed users into the brand.
- Cements loyalty among core family target.
- Steals share from other bread with a higher margin offer.
- Builds brand goodness associations.

See also: Coke Zero.

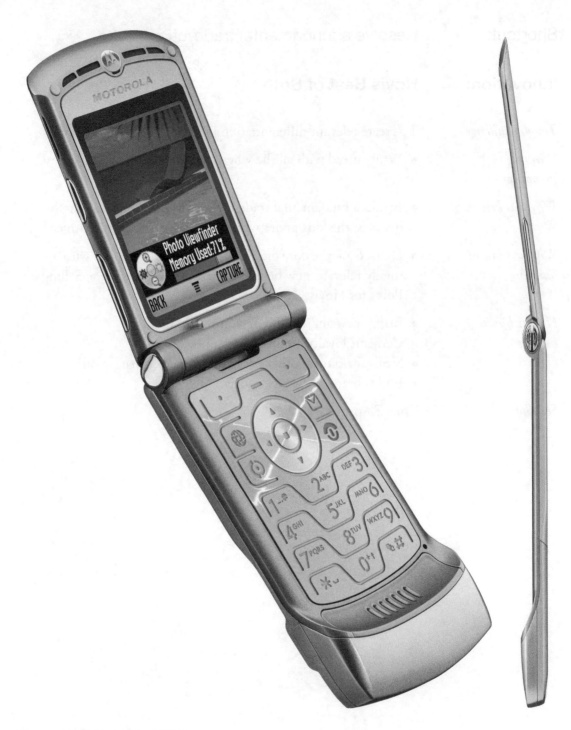

Figure 10.4: Motorola RAZR.

Shortcut:	Never underestimate the power of design

Innovation:	**Motorola RAZR**

Tough challenge Reinvigorate a stale brand in the world's fastest moving consumer technology market against global giants and major new entrants.

Winning proposition
- A super-slim, super light phone that does what you want it to do most; make calls and look cool.

Why it is better
- The first phone that married great design with good functionality. This was a phone with few compromises and that's what made it so unique and impactful in the marketplace.

Why it is brand building
- Revolutionized the market when no one thought it needed it.
- Made Motorola not just cool but the coolest most fashionable brand in an image-obsessed category.

How it builds business
- Has put Motorola back on the map as a top consideration brand, enabling their offer to be successfully widened with other models.

See also: Apple iPod Nano.

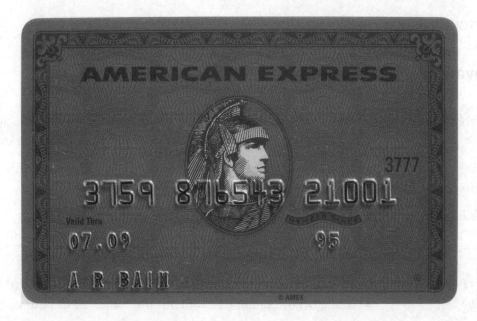

Figure 10.5: American Express Red.

Shortcut:	When everyone else zigs, zag

Innovation: **American Express Red**

Tough challenge

Create relevant differentiation and growth for an established but stagnating behemoth of a brand in a hugely crowded price obsessed low margin category.

Winning proposition

- Join Bono in making poverty history: with every purchase you make we give a percentage to fight poverty.

Why it is better

- Turns the very cornerstone of capitalism, the transaction, into a positive statement about global politics.
- Resegments a commoditized category to create new growth.

Why it is brand building

- Leverages the brand's premium status into a unique and differentiating stance – only Amex could get Bono.
- Does something so opposite to the brand's 1980's, Gordon Gekko, big business roots that it instantly brings it bang up to date and back in line with today's jeans-wearing 30-something CEOs.

How it builds business

- Targets new users with something other than undifferentiated low rates, driving share.
- Connects into a whole 'movement' that takes it outside existing channels, e.g. mobile phone stores with the Motorola Red phone

See also: Toyota Prius.

Figure 10.6: Renault Scenic.

Shortcut:	Break category rules

Innovation: **Renault Scenic (1999)**

Tough challenge	To make a family car that's genuinely different (not a regular estate/wagon or a people-carrying bus)
Winning proposition	• The first car that's actually designed around a family's needs to the last detail; higher rear seats, loads of storage, truly easily reconfigurable, mirrors to see the kids not just the road etc.
Why it is better	• Breaks the category rules by treating the rear seats as more important than the front seats, just like parents do.
Why it is brand building	• So strong a proposition it usurped its Megane sub-branding and became a leading brand in its own right. • Demonstrates true consumer insight that has rubbed off on the entire range.
How it builds business	• Brought back a whole generation of people to the brand who left when they grew out of their Clios.
See also:	Volvic Touch of Fruit.

Figure 10.7: Johnson's Holiday Skin™ Body Lotion.

Shortcut:	Create hybrids to build new categories

Innovation:	**Johnson's Holiday Skin™ Body Lotion**

Tough challenge

Generate growth in the crowded & highly competitive body moisturiser market from a leading brand that already has all the bases covered

Winning proposition

- Body moisturiser that delivers a light tan 365 days a year.

Why it is better

- *Q:* Is it fake tan or a body lotion?
- *A:* Neither – it's a damn good idea; body lotion that subtly brings you an everyday golden glow.

Why it is brand building

- Demonstrates true consumer insight. Brings a relevant differentiated benefit into a crowded market.

How it builds business

- Drives repeat purchase through the desire to maintain a year round tan.
- Trades loyal consumers up to a more premium offer.

See also:

Becel/Flora Pro-Activ.

Figure 10.8: Yoplait Petits Filous Frubes.

Shortcut:	Deliver extraordinary convenience

Innovation: **Yoplait Petits Filous Frubes**

Tough challenge   To break out of the stagnant kids 'dessert' occasion and into the growth areas of on-the-go snacking and lunchboxes.

Winning proposition
- The delicious yoghurt kids can eat without a spoon (and if you freeze it – it will stay cool till lunchtime).

Why it is better
- No spoon required, thus opens the way to be eaten as a snack.
- Just the right size and amount; other pouches were too much for little kids to handle.

Why it is brand building
- Leverages the trusted taste and goodness of Petits Filous into the growing on-the-go snacking area.
- Brings fresh fun and dynamism into the brand.

How it builds business
- Dramatically increases the possible snacking occasions for the brand.
- Gets into totally new occasions: lunchboxes.
- Harnesses pester power to drive repeat purchase - what Mum used to choose for them, kids now ask for themselves.

See also: Tampax Compak.

Figure 10.9: Gü Desserts.

Shortcut:	Premiumize a commoditized category

New Brand: **Gü Desserts**

Tough challenge	Enter the crowded, low value, own-label-dominated desserts market, with an unbeatable 'gold standard' of home-made, and create a cut through proposition.
Winning proposition	• Quick and easy, good as home-made little chocolate puds with a tangibly quirky personality that taps directly into the mega-trend of foodies without the time to cook.
	• They clearly believe that nothing in life is as heart-warmingly gorgeous as a proper chocolate pud. . . and a lot of people agree!
Why it is better:	• They have taken contemporary restaurant codes into a dead category with microwaveable simplicity.
Why it is brand building	• This is a highly focused offer with a strong personality and no matter how hard own-label try, they can never be as expert nor develop as personal a relationship in just one (minor) category.
How it builds business	• The little glass ramekins they come in get washed and put in the cupboard to be used later. They become permanent repeat purchase reminders.
See also:	Innocent Smoothies.

Figure 10.10: Ocado Online Grocery.

Shortcut:	Add service in a commodity market

New Brand: **Ocado Online Grocery**

Tough challenge	Create relevant motivating differentiation in a huge commodity market (or you'll sink without a trace).
Winning proposition	• Deliver to a 1-hour prearranged time slot, because your time is precious. • Deliver Waitrose (premium) groceries only.
Why it is better	• They manage to stick to 1-hour timeslots. No one else can. • They understand that the consumer's time is more precious than theirs
Why it is brand building	• Just this little difference has created a whole premium brand. For more upscale consumers the hassle of having to stay in for half a day to wait for your groceries is not worth it so they don't bother. • Ocado creates its own market.
How it builds business	• Brings in consumers who wouldn't use normal online grocers. • Successfully targets high value consumers.
See also:	Virgin Atlantic.

The Practicalities

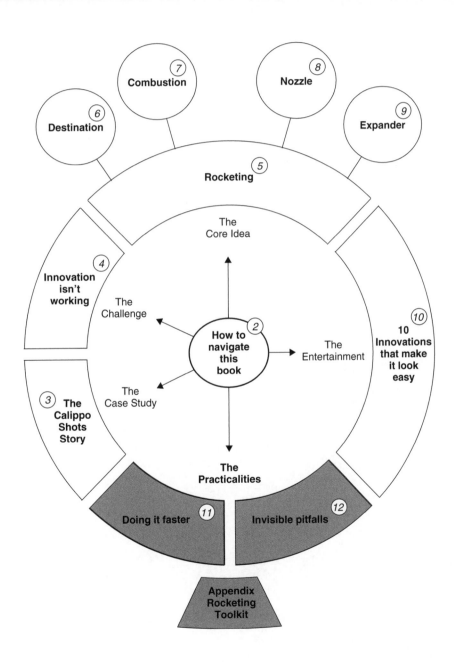

PART V

"The big don't always eat the small. The fast always catch the slow."

 Headlines

In today's fast-moving markets, doing innovation projects significantly faster but just as effectively would deliver considerable benefits. There are five key factors that can increase speed without affecting quality: planning decisions in advance, keeping to small teams, doing multiple brainstorming in parallel, getting insight in real time, and using fast agencies. Together they could mean that a typical 12-month process could be completed in 8 weeks.

It always takes longer than you want it to

Along with traffic jams, dentistry and chilling a bottle of good white wine, innovation always takes longer than you'd hope. Surely in this day and age an innovation can't take that long to get from ideation to the market? If we can get a diesel car to go at over 560 km per hour, and get a mortgage approved in 30 minutes – things that only a few years ago seemed destined to be forever slow – then surely major multinationals with all their might and manpower can get a banana-flavoured yoghurt onto a supermarket shelf in under a year? But experience suggests that, unless you own the shelf in question, it's a very hard thing to do. And to stand any chance of success you have to make the initial innovation project run to weeks, not months.

Speed thrills

Doing innovation faster ought to be one of the must-do initiatives for most major branded businesses. This is a key success factor for tomorrow's winning brands. The relevance and consumer motivation of an idea and the quality of the product have long since been drivers of eventual success. Today, however, for everything from toothbrushes to tomato sauce, the speed with which you deliver it to market has moved from 'important' to 'bloody essential' on the consumer's list of brand choice drivers. It's no longer just mobile phone makers and fashionistas who have to worry about hitting the shelves on time or hitting the bin. Beating your competitors, including the retailers, is important. Beating the consumer's expectations is positively differentiating. For the next decade there should be a reworking of the Gordon Gekko 80's mantra of 'greed is good': Today, speed is good.

Fashion on speed

Zara has built a pan-European fashion business from the ground up, not in decades but in a few short years, based on speed. They can design, manufacture and supply to the shelves of their stores a new range in a matter of weeks. What takes their competitors months to do, they accomplish seemingly overnight. And it's not only those consumers who normally buy cheaply who love it. Why would fashion victims who can afford premium brands buy cheap? Because not only can they get the very latest fashions fastest this way but they can also ensure that they stay at the leading edge by getting them twice as often. Zara have made speed of innovation a consumer relevant competitive edge.

Case Study: Project Blues for Unilever Foods

'Blues' was the code name for a 2006 Unilever project to create new ideas for chilled foods. The remit was broad; snacks, main meals, hot and cold food and drinks – all were under consideration.

The challenge? To do it differently in order to avoid seeing out a full 12 months before anything useful emerged. The Brandgym was asked to design the process and challenge the team to deliver 2–3 fully worked up ideas that met the clear brief shown below.

Project Blues Brief

Create 2–3 concepts, with prototypes and initial marketing mixes that are:

- Motivating and differentiated for real consumers
- Leveraging product development expertise
- Manufacturable in principle (from an R&D point of view)
- With a feasible but new packaging idea
- Strong fit to one of Unilever's core food brands

And all of this in just 8 weeks. A 'drop-deadline' was set for a presentation to senior management of a concept, packaging, product prototype and initial design at a big meeting already in the calendar.

The Approach

Using Rocketing principles we designed a process that took only 8 weeks to deliver concepts that met the brief (Figure 11.1). It involved multiple sources of insights drawn from far and wide, including the best of the thinking and ideas that already existed across several recent projects. There were multiple ideation sessions to increase both the quality and quantity of ideas, built around two real-time consumer insight sessions. All this was run in parallel with developing initial business cases for each idea, as well as working with a design agency to build the ideas into initial in-store mixes.

Principles for speed

The following are tried, tested and practical, change-it-right-now ways to improve the time-to-delivery of your current innovation projects:

- Plan in decisions

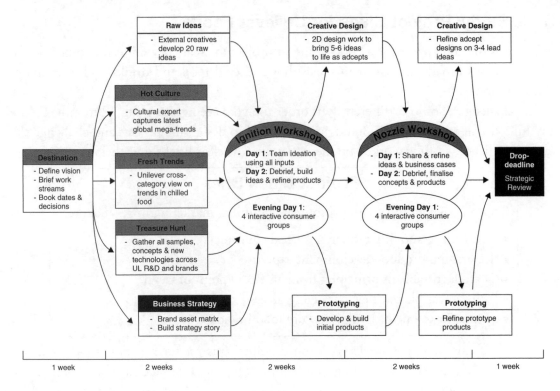

Figure 11.1: Project Blues 8-week innovation process.

- Smaller teams
- Parallel ideation
- Real time insight
- Fast agencies

Plan in decisions

Welcome to the biggest single time waster in innovation. It's a fact that when it comes to any project, decision taking chews up most of time. The need for taking decisions–a good many decisions–along the way of any innovation project is unavoidable. Wasting time doing so is not. The trick is to clearly identify the decisions that need to be taken at each key stage, plan them in at the appropriate juncture, then take them quickly. Failure to do so simply ensures that delays mushroom out of control further down the track. How many times have you been in a seemingly efficient and focused meeting only to come out thinking "What did we actually decide?". Too often the decision made in the meeting is "We need to discuss that". Everyone nods sagely and you move on to the next topic. No decision has been taken;

Box 11.1: The Quick Decision	
MD:	I need speed on this one, Simpkins.
Simpkins:	Understood.
MD:	The CEO has his eyes on this and the board has made it a top priority, so we need to move fast.
Simpkins:	I take it there's budget?
MD:	Blank cheque on this one.
Simpkins:	I'll get the briefs out this afternoon.
MD:	Excellent. Just as soon as the CEO approves the process.
Simpkins:	Oh?
MD:	And the FD wants to personally check there's enough resource allocated. . .
Simpkins:	But. . .
MD:	And the rest of the board all want to OK the plan too, as it's so very important.
Simpkins :	How quickly can we do that?
MD:	Top of the agenda at the next board meeting, in 3 months.
Simpkins:	3 months!
MD:	If we miss the launch window, it'll be on your head Simpkins.
Simpkins:	(Gulp.)
MD:	Good man.

you have merely recognized that one needs to be made, and valuable time has been wasted. Identifying the decisions that need to be taken, however small, and planning them in well in advance is the key to taking them on time and freeing up the rest of the process. Senior decisions, particularly the small ones, seem to be the most injurious, as Simpkins finds out in Box 11.1.

Tackling decision making

- Know when you need the big cheese and plan in 15 minutes with the all-knowing PA.
- Start meetings with 'What decisions do we need to take?' List them and then check back to make sure you've addressed them all.
- When you take your seniors, or anyone for that matter, through a status update on your project, be clear to indicate the decisions you need from them up front.

Blues: Decision planning

There were three specific sessions planned in with senior management along the way. Because the process was quick, it was especially important that we got senior input just when we needed it and kept them comfortable with the development of the ideas as we sped along. The three sessions were:

1 Right at the start to understand their hunches and initial ideas, as well as to recheck our approach was going to deliver to the business' strategic needs.
2 Just before our second workshop to share where we had got to and get feedback on both concept and product directions.
3 At the end, the day before the deadline, to give real confidence that both our ideas and products were set to wow the next day at the strategic review.

We prepared the senior executives for each of these sessions, carefully explaining what we were going to show them and, critically, what kind of feedback we were looking for. Avoiding giving them any nasty surprises ensured that we received no game-stopping feedback from them.

Smaller teams

It always starts out so well. Just a few of you from marketing, R&D and Insight. Three key people running a nice tight project. And then it happens. Little by little, one by one, the team grows. So-and-so from the agency ought to be involved; R&D insist on the functional specialist tagging along throughout "not on the team, you understand, just there at every meeting"; finance need to be kept in the loop. And before you know it the inexorable swelling of numbers ensures that each meeting involves at least 10 people and meetings slip back weeks simply by trying to find dates when most people can attend. So how big (or small) is the ideal team in a large company? Realistically these can rarely be as small as three (though, if you see it's a possibility, go for it). In circumstances involving multiple countries or a global representation, five or six is more usual, but even sticking to this number can prove a real challenge.

Sticking to smaller teams

- Decide up front how big you want the team to be and stick to it. Make it very clear to everyone that keeping the team small is an important success factor for the project.

- Write good meeting reports and send them out the next day without fail. Focus on the actions, responsibilities and timings, not the classical minutes of a meeting. This is a good task for a project assistant or innovation agency.
- Be clear that the worst way to keep people up to speed on a project is to have them sit in on meetings. Extra bodies clog up meetings and dissipate energy and focus. If people want to be kept 'in the loop' then send them the meeting report the day after each meeting.
- Plan in update sessions with key stakeholders; even 15-minute sessions can work very well. This is so much better than creating a larger meeting that takes ages to plan, creates delays and brings unnecessary stress for the team.

The benefits of smaller teams

- *Easier to fix meetings*: Fewer diaries to manage.
- *Quicker meetings*: Less time taken to share everyone's thinking.
- *Helps you take decisions more quickly*: It's obvious when you all agree.
- *Keeps you focused*: Less opportunity for factions to develop or parts of the team to have different perspectives on core issues. You have to argue things out there and then and move on.
- *More accountability*: When things happen, it's obvious who is responsible so you don't have to ask. This focuses people's actions and ensures fewer mistakes through lack of attention to details. When your job is on the line you take more care.

Blues: Small team

The team was kept small throughout the project, even though it had a high profile in a large organization and went across many geographies and brands. The team and their relevant responsibilities were:

- Project Leader: Overall direction, decision making, managing stakeholders.
- Project Manager: Planning, budgets, ideas and international liaison.
- Technical Lead: Overall product delivery, interfacing with technical specialists.
- Consultant: Process design and facilitation, ideas, strategic input, creative output management.

By virtue of moving fast, any attempts at adding people to the team did not work. What did happen is that people who wanted to get involved were invited to attend workshops if the team believed they brought valuable new perspectives and experiences. If this wasn't the case, they were put on the circulation list for meeting reports and 'fyi' concept updates. Because it was always very clear who the core team was, they were able to take strong uncontested ownership of the project. This helped enormously in clearing the way to move with speed. If you stay small and plan well, you can move quickly.

Parallel Ideation

Doing things simultaneously is a great way to speed up: you halve the number of output meetings and status sessions you need as things come together naturally or feed directly into other sessions without the need for a formal debrief and then subsequent re-presenting. Hosting multiple ideation sessions in parallel massively increases the bandwidth of the creativity you are getting. Two of the key Rocketing principles laid out in Chapter 7 come into play here too:

- *External creatives*: Making sure that you do not just have the usual suspects sitting around the room when you start to ideate on this new project. Getting external creatives to develop ideas from their relative naivety hugely enhances your team's creativity. It opens avenues of thought that everyday brand management tends to close off.
- *3 Bucket Principle*: Enabling a thorough collation of all concepts and ideas that exist in and around your business in other brand teams, countries and projects so that you can start with a bucket load of ideas, not a blank sheet of paper.

Blues: Multi-parallel ideation

The process undertaken utilized all of these approaches and built a multi-parallel process that navigated quickly through eight separate idea-creating sessions in only a few days. This meant that there was a huge bandwidth of creativity in the project, with plenty of room for silly ideas (of which there were quite a few) as well as radical ideas. This gave the team a tremendous level of confidence that they were going to deliver, and thus the freedom to change things even at the last minute. The ideation steps were:

- Raw ideas created by external creatives as an input to stretch thinking in the first workshop. Twenty ideas were delivered, each on a single A4 as hand-drawn illustrated simple concepts (see Figure 11.2).
- Team ideation session during Day 1 of the first workshop that used various inputs as idea fuel to create an initial set of rough concepts:

Route5 **Frookies** Fresh Fruit Dough Cookies

So good they're frookin' freaky!

Fresh baked light cake/cookie dough packed with fresh fruit pieces.
Lunch box Frookies - 2 x 4cm dia

100% Natural
No Added Anything
No Nasties

Two Frookies = one of your 5-a-day

• Raspberry & Fresh Mint
• Peach
• Apricot
• Delicious, light and made with fresh eggs

Find them in the chiller cabinet
Eat now or warm for 10mins

Figure 11.2: A raw idea from external creatives.

- 20 raw ideas from external creatives
- Trends and expert insight
- 30+ ideas gathered from other projects, R&D experiments and local country initiatives
- Competitive trawl.
- An interactive real-time consumer session in the evening of the first day of the workshop. The team continued creating ideas as they listened to and interacted with consumers over the initial set of rough concepts.
- Team ideation session based on the instant debrief of the consumer's reaction to the initial rough concepts.
- The creative design agency's input in turning the revised set of concepts into colourful adcepts with pack mock-ups.
- The second workshop discussing the same sequence of: ideation, real-time consumer interaction and further ideation the next day. In particular the final refinement being done in-situ by one half of the team while the other discussed and refined the business cases.
- The creative design agency's further input in designing new adcepts and pack mock-ups based on the finalized concepts coming from the second workshop.

Real-time insight

As we have seen, this is a powerful ingredient in the 'doing it faster' mix. Garnering insight in real time means bringing consumers right into the middle of your ideation session and exposing the ideas to them as they occur. Getting feedback while creating ideas blends the refinement process with the creative one. By working with consumers like this you eliminate the need for extensive concept crafting at early stages; you have to go with what you've got. The other benefit of doing insight in real time is that your interaction with consumers becomes a discussion, not a simple question and answer session. This changes the dynamic between marketer and buyer; you are serving them, almost as if you were greeting them in your shop. This is a very conducive relationship for creating and refining ideas.

What you gain

- *Real speed*: You can do in one night that which takes two months to do through normal qualitative research.
- *More truthful reactions*: Consumers are evaluating the offers more as they would in real life; quickly and looking at the whole mix – pack, product and idea. Reactions like "I just don't like it" challenge the team to think "why?" and solve it right there and then with the consumer in front of them.
- *Instant rewrites*: You can try stuff out there and then; redraft your idea as you sit there and see what they think.
- *Fuller feedback*: You can explore the core idea, language, packaging, product and more all at the same time as consumers are reacting to it more like a real offer.

What you lose

- *Detailed feedback*: As the discussion is flying so fast there is no way the moderators can take in and analyse the detail, as they do in a standard focus group. It is there to spur new ideas, not to get an evaluative analysis of your concepts.
- *Written reports*: The key output of the session is the thoughts it inspires and the concepts that you rewrite. What you get is an instant download from the moderators the next morning, not a glossy report. This is NOT research. This is inspiration.

Blues: Real-time consumer workouts

During this eight-week project there was no formal qualitative exploration of the concepts. This would have taken the full eight weeks just in itself. However, the brief was to demonstrate that the ideas had consumer appeal – the approach was to work with consumers throughout the process. As shown in the overall workplan above, two real-time consumer 'workouts' were planned for the middle evening of each two-day workshop. Each session was set up with the following:

- Four different groups of consumers (four in each, 16 in total)
- Four moderators
- A huge array of packaging stimulus from all kinds of products across food and non-food
- Prototype product samples (perfectly edible, naturally)
- The core team, plus relevant technical specialists.

Each moderator was given four adcept boards and corresponding short written concepts to work with. The consumers spent half an hour with each moderator, rotating so that they saw all the concepts and each moderator saw all the consumers. The team were encouraged to talk to and discuss the ideas with the consumers. The effect was tremendously stimulating and effective in moving the team's thinking forward very quickly. The next day everyone had fresh thoughts on how to improve each idea and the R&D team had a clear steer on the direction in which to take the product and packaging. And all completed in just 24 hours.

Fast agencies

When speed is of the essence and you're doing everything humanly possible (and, quite possibly, inhumanly) to expedite every stage of the process, the last thing you need is to be slowed to a walking pace by an agency. If you're not careful, even well-meaning and seemingly well-organized organizations can precipitate the dreaded parachute effect on your process. Don't let them. Just ensure that the freefall is controlled and you know (roughly) where you're going to land. One way to dramatically improve your chances of making this happen is to **use smaller agencies** who can give you dedicated resources rather than bigger ones where your concepts go into the system and wait their turn to secure designer and Mac operator time. You'll also know exactly who you're working with at every stage as it will very likely be the same person. This makes it easier to strike up a good working relationship, allowing you to ensure that they manage their workload to fit into your timescale. Another way is to **demand quicker turnarounds**. Simple but very effective.

Blues: Fast design

We hired a dedicated innovation design agency that turned around concepts to an incredibly high standard in just 1–2 days each time. We briefed them on exactly what we needed so they were able to book their resources in advance and invited them to turn up at 5 pm on the second day of each two-day workshop and briefed them directly. Keeping the concepts to A3 avoided long print times and reduced the likelihood of printer trouble. Copy changes could be achieved in a matter of minutes as all that was required was to type in the rewrites and hit 'print'. Crucially, even though packs bearing brand names were being shown in photorealistic colour to consumers, the team was crystal clear that this was not design development so no designs needed to be signed off or to cohere with any design guidelines.

Blues: The result

The project was very successful and delivered bang on the nail within eight weeks. The reaction internally was a mixture of delight and surprise: 'It would normally take us 8–12 months to deliver ideas of this quality and to this level of finish. This is amazing.' Just be aware that a project such as this is only the first stage of innovation; there is still plenty of scope for the ideas to get caught in a 'strategy jam' and lose all the pace they were given at their initial development.

Key takeouts

- Innovation can be done considerably faster and you don't have to compromise quality to achieve it.
- Decision making is the single biggest cause of time delays in innovation. Plan in key decisions from the start.
- Getting real insight for ideas doesn't have to take full-scale research. Quick, real-time inputs can deliver what you need instantly.
- Don't let team size get out of hand – when forming innovation teams, small is beautiful.
- Innovation doesn't have to be sequential. Doing steps in parallel increases speed and diversity.
- Don't just accept the status quo, work with agencies who can handle high-speed turnarounds.

Checklist: Doing it faster

	Yes	*No*
Have you planned in the necessary decisions in advance?	☐	☐
Is your team small, fixed and clear on their responsibilities?	☐	☐

	Yes	*No*
• Have you planned your ideation sessions in parallel?	☐	☐
• Is much of your initial insight planned in to happen in 'real time'?	☐	☐
• Have you agreed fast turnaround times for stimulus with your agency?	☐	☐

 ## Handover

We have seen how to speed up a typical innovation project, without losing the quality of ideas. The next step in looking at the practicalities of Rocketing innovation is to consider the pitfalls that lie along the way, and how to avoid them.

Avoiding the pitfalls

"Innovation isn't difficult because employees don't have good ideas. Rather, myriad
obstacles in the idea-to-cash process limit a company's ability to innovate."

Howard Smith

 Headlines

Innovation is strewn with pitfalls for the unwary to fall into. They appear in many guises
and are often well meant, but are nonetheless deadly. From the product under-delivering

and the 'not invented here' syndrome to just plain giving up, they are all things that the innovator needs to be aware of and build in some simple but effective avoidance strategies.

Pitfalls and Pratfalls

Innovation is creation, but it is also packed with pitfalls and pratfalls. Around the corner of every great idea lurks a banana skin for the unwary. Somehow innovation is all too easily stifled in big organizations. Smothered, it seems (often with good intentions) until it stops breathing completely. We have seen (1) that the innovation funnel can hinder more than it helps; (2) that too much focus on radical innovation throws open the portals to the weird and wonderful but does not deliver on the core business challenges; (3) that focusing heaps of attention on incremental varianting makes marketers miss the bigger picture; and (4) that the mono-mentality of working project by project rather than seeing your entire year's work as an integrated idea producing engine, produces a micro approach to innovation which gets less output from more input.

These are the quicksands of innovation. But negotiating these is only half the battle. You still need to remain vigilant for the host of other pernicious innovation pitfalls prevalent in large organizations, and these are the most difficult to avoid since they are mostly invisible and appear totally benign when they occur. How do you side-step a man-trap you can't even see? Or dance around a landmine disguised as a creative rose bed? If you stumble upon an oasis in an innovation desert how can you be certain it's not just a mirage? The fist step is **recognition**.

First, it should be noted that these pitfalls are usually well intentioned, derived from good sources and good backgrounds, and are offered as helpful additions to the innovation process. Their creators are often unaware of their destructive capabilities and they are not wrought on the project with a view to stifling it – indeed quite the reverse is true – hence their ability to quietly mask insight, to gently distract and to subtly procrastinate, before wrestling every ounce of creativity to the ground and beating it over the head with a very large hammer. Little wonder then that they ultimately blunt the impact of good ideas! Good intentions are all very well but it's good execution that counts. Lose that along the way and what started out as positive inputs end up killing as effectively as strong bleach (see Figure 12.1).

Figure 12.1: Invisible pitfalls.

Nine innovation pitfalls

Table 12.1 shows a summary of nine pitfalls and the suggested avoidance strategies.

No. 1: Oops, the product is useless

Bigger, better, bolder... nonsense

The most common reason for an innovation to fail is that the product simply does not live up to the claim bestowed on it. Consumers are told that this new version will 'taste better', 'last longer', 'feel softer', 'save you time', 'improve your health' – and in 8 out of 10 instances, it just doesn't.

Table 12.1: Nine innovation pitfalls.

Pitfall	Avoidance Strategy
1. Oops, the product is useless	• Clear, consumer relevant action standards • Get R&D involved right from the start • Prototype early • Try the product out with real people early on
2. 'Not invented here' syndrome	• Evaluate using Idea Power matrices, for objectivity • Reward people for bringing ideas from outside • Rewrite other's ideas in your own style before using them
3. The 'could it be' killer	• Stick to your original vision • Credit the team with ideas, not individuals
4. Over-testing	• Stick to your plan • Just say 'no'
5. Killing by proxy	• Use naïve resources • Don't take it for granted, challenge the killer-by-proxy • Let consumers be the judge
6. The off-guard boss	• Plan in a quickie, don't take them by surprise • Stay regular, keep to your review timings
7. 'Yes, but'-ters	• Install a 'Yes, but…' swear box in your meeting rooms • Use 'Yes, and..' as a permanent replacement
8. Poor casting	• Write briefs for each innovation role and cast to them • Build a team for the quantity of sparks that fly
9. Giving up	• Do a Dyson – have faith, persevere and never give up • Create your own kind of test

Over-zealous claiming

Another common fault. The problem here usually stems from a requirement that the written concept must beat existing claims in the marketplace to be given the go ahead. There is a seemingly endless succession of concept testing rounds with increasingly elaborate (and hard to justify) claims. When they do finally hit the shelves consumers can easily reject an underlyingly strong idea because, to paraphrase Shakespeare, the consumer, "doth protest too much".

Boo boo

A famous example at the time of the dot.com bubble was Boo.com. This was an ambitious business plan to create the first online designer clothing retailer. In principle it was a good idea. That's why it was funded to the hilt with millions of dollars which the team duly burned through in spectacular fashion. Why did it fail? It claimed to make clothes shopping easier. It didn't. Broadband connection speeds were still years away and the site was so overloaded with imagery and 360° clothes viewing it took an age for every page to load at dial-up speeds. In other words, the product simply didn't meet the claim.

Making a silk purse out of a sow's ear

This is a task often given to R&D teams – not literally of course (that would be silly) but in effect that is what it amounts to. Limited product development resources or insufficient time to develop a new product – or both – will almost inevitably increase your likelihood of failure. Better yet is R&D being told to add in the amazing new ingredient/product but without any additional cost. This means that their hands are tied from the get–go and only enough 'magic dust' is put into the product to register a difference in the lab – good enough for a claim in an ad, but undetectable by consumers. This is an almost premeditated form of failure in innovation.

As an example, just look at any category that has 'new and improved' flashes on key brands. Large R&D projects have no doubt been instigated to reformulate the product with the clear view that consumers will instantly notice the change and will stampede the aisles to get their hands on it. In reality consumers barely even register this kind of improvement.

Avoid beige

The beige of innovation is the arguably the most difficult of them all to spot as it isn't a clear failure – it simply doesn't succeed on any level! It is the nondescript entity that does what it set out to do (just), works (barely), and ticks all the requisite boxes (in *very* faint pencil). The result? It ends up completely underwhelming people and totally undermining the very reason it was put into the market in the first place.

Take Gizmondo. This was a valiant European attempt to compete with Sony and Nintendo in the fast-growing mobile gaming market. On paper this snappily named mobile gadget had it all – GPS, VGA Camera, SMS, MMS and Email comms, MP3, WAV and Midi music, WMV and Mpeg4 video – as impressive an array of three-letter acronyms as any other product. So how could it fail? Well, on almost every dimension. It never stood a chance from the consumer's perspective. Versus mobile phones, it couldn't make or receive calls and versus the mobile gaming platforms it had the biggest Achilles' heel of all – no good games. A key selling point for Gizmondo was unique games which used GPS to identify players' actual locations in real time and use this data as part of the gameplay experience – a very innovative idea – but game developers didn't buy into it, leaving an embarrassing dearth of games. Crucially, consumers didn't understand who it was aimed at, exactly how to use it, or why they should buy it. So they didn't.

Avoidance strategies

- *Clear, consumer-relevant action standards*: These should be set up at the start of the innovation process as part of your vision: e.g. 'Ordinary people should tell us unprompted that it's softer/tastier/easier. . . on first using the product.'
- *Get R&D involved right at the start* – not just at the product briefing stage. Give them more time to harness their technical know-how to address all the challenges that crop up along the way, rather than face them all at once at a later stage.
- *Try the product out with real people early on* – not just with experts and stakeholders, or in the lab. Real people give real feedback and there is no replacement for it. Don't leave it until the usage test to find out what they really think.
- *Prototype early*: Build an example of the product in question, even if it's only rough. The feedback you get will be that much more accurate, and useful. Just ask James Dyson, Art Fry, Steve Jobs or the CEO of L'Oréal.

Why not. . .
ask R&D how they would go about doubling the performance for half the cost?

- Don't worry, they won't lynch you – the trick is to imagine the factory had burned to the ground and they could start again, designing everything from scratch. A useful exercise to clarify vision and execution – or even a plan to carry out if the project is sufficiently large. It's a crazy idea but it might just work. . . (factory burning optional).

No. 2: 'Not invented here' syndrome

Widely reported and well known among business executives the world over, this syndrome is still virulent and alive in most large organizations. Its power to abort good ideas at an embryonic stage is superseded only by its chameleon-like ability to adopt disguises to match its environment. Indeed, you may have already experienced it without even realizing it. Some of its favourite masks include the local market favourites of 'We know better', 'Our issues are different' or even the seemingly innocuous (or more dangerous still, seemingly well-meaning and helpful) 'How can we improve on this?'. But look beneath the surface and you'll find that these can all too often be unmasked as aggressive and dangerous forms of 'We want to come up with our own solutions if it's all the same with you'. This is the 'Not invented here' syndrome at work.

Going glocal

The most widespread of these is the **global-local** variant. Picture the scene – global delivers a new innovation idea, fully tested in agreed representative markets. Local market is fully involved in the global process from the outset and agrees to 'look at it' for launch. Three months later local market tests are carried out and, surprise, surprise, a totally different concept has won through. Inevitably logical rationales are wielded: 'It just wasn't cutting through with our consumers', 'We've refined it for our market' – but the truth is that there was never the intention to make it work in the first place.

For example, consider The Yoghurt Files – innovations from a fictitious global dairy company shown in Figures 12.2 and 12.3.

The Yoghurt Files

Figure 12.2: A harmonized global innovation idea.

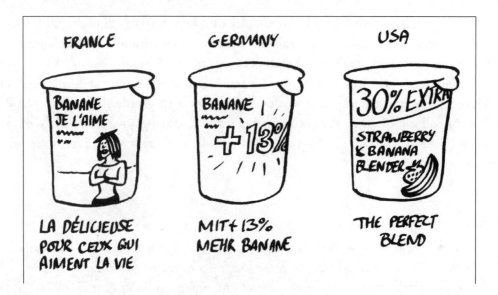

Figure 12.3: A 'not-invented-here' global innovation idea.

Going clobal

The other side of the coin is the equally damaging **local-global** variant which is seen less often but its potential to stifle good ideas at birth is alarming. A local country comes up with a terrific innovation that cracks a major problem and offers it up in a global meeting – only to find every other region giving any number of reasons why they will not even try it out in their market. The result? A local market that will be very reluctant to offer any more ideas, and a global problem that remains unresolved.

Avoidance strategies

- *Idea Power* evaluation techniques are a simple yet powerful way to review, as objectively as possible; new ideas that come from a different source. Make the use of this a standard part of your innovation process.
- *Reward people* for bringing in ideas from outside sources. This is the start of an 'open source' innovation policy that is at the root of increasing the quality and quantity of ideas available to you for each innovation challenge.
- *Rewrite other's ideas* in your own style/handwriting before presenting them to your team (simple but effective!).

If you look at successful global innovators there is seldom a chance for local markets to redefine or reinvent an idea. Their role is simply to make the best of the global idea in their market. Can you imagine the French Apple marketing Director saying 'We can't pronounce iPod in France, so we called it 'Vive la Musique Jouer'?' Somehow I don't think Mr Jobs would respect that point of view too much!

No. 3: The 'could it be. . . ?' killer

Sad but true, over-eagerness to improve and refine an idea can all too quickly eschew the very reason for its existence in the first place. Couple this with an infectious enthusiasm from the team to own it and you have a serial idea killer.

Similar to the 'Not invented here' syndrome, and just as virulent, but in some ways harder to stop – after all, who wants to curb enthusiasm from their team, either for seemingly great new builds or for ownership? Imagine the scene . . . your big new concept has just proved a real hit with consumers; you decide to gather together the wider development team and present it to them. Everyone gets very excited by this new idea and positive vibes and energy are ricocheting around the room.

> "This is great! Could it be done in a version for kids?"
> "Yeah! Could we do it in black?"
> "We could target football fans if we did it with club logos!"
> "This is fantastic – if it was bigger and easier to open it could be great for older people. We have a sales team focused on that channel!"
> "Oh, we've just got to do an on-the-go version for hectic Mums."

Each of these ideas is received by the room with enthusiastic approval since everyone loves a successful idea. Particularly if it's theirs. More and more builds are thrown in at an ever-accelerating rate driven by the passionate vibes quickly created by team brainstorms and, by the end, the marketing manager has so many different nuances and variations of the original concept to contend with he/she simply doesn't know which way is up any longer. The manager is then tasked with 'tweaking' the concept to broaden it so that it can encompass all these excellent ideas. . .

The net result is that the nice clean focused concept that did so well has been watered down and blunted to incorporate all the new directions, leaving only a murky mess of half ideas swamped by derivatives. This is the 'Could it be?' killer at work. And it's an almost invisible killer. It comes from a very good place: excitement at a good new idea; enthusiasm to make it better still; and the desire to be part of the team that made it great. And it's all the more deadly for that.

> *But hang on a minute – surely building fresh thinking into ideas and expanding them to create maximum impact at launch is the key to successful innovation?*

Indeed it is, and continuous ideas building is good discipline. But it must be channelled within a tight supportive and protective framework, particularly early on in the process. It is most important at the later stage (Expander) than at the earlier idea creation and development (Combustion) stage. If you let your idea get swamped by over-zealous builders you will end up with a bucket of slop, not a set of sharp new ideas.

Consider the simple innovation from our fictitious dairy company shown in Figure 12.4.

The Yoghurt Files

Figure 12.4: A new innovation.

Now add in some enthusiastic builds. . .

Builds	*Concept refinement*
For the health conscious	– watered down so only half the calories
For teenagers	– with a strong caffeine boost
For kids	– small pots with a 'Banana-man' character
For people on the go	– drinkable yoghurt, no need for a spoon
For people who don't like bananas	– Only a hint of banana for a very mild taste

The result: A small, watery, tasteless, over caffeinated, artificially sweet, Banana-man franchise fee-requiring expensive yoghurt for everybody, that no-one wants.

Avoidance strategies

- *Stick to your vision*: Ensure that the whole team understands the clearly defined vision for the product – who is it targeting? Why does it work? What makes it different and better? Then refer to the vision regularly during the builds stage to ensure that any builds really are just that – and not an inadvertent wrecking ball to the concept.
- *Team as originator*: Be very clear that any ideas will be credited to the team as a whole, regardless of who voiced them (this makes perfect sense since most ideas are actually builds on other suggestions anyway). So fight the urge to say 'This was Jack's idea' when you present it at the board meeting, and take a more inclusive tone and credit the idea to 'The team'. People will then be less inclined to justify their place on the team by having one of their ideas 'chosen'.

No. 4: Over-testing

This is an easy pitfall to stumble into when time is on your side (as it occasionally is!), and is most commonly characterized by the phrase "mmm. . . let's do a few more groups", which itself is often preceded by the phrase "What was our evaluation criteria again?" and often followed by "Shit, can anyone remember why we are going down this route?! How are we going to justify the expense? What have we got to show for all the time? Wait a minute, I've got it – let's do a few more. . . ." But in all seriousness (that was) the desire to engage in round upon round of testing is usually meant with positive intent, a desire to dig a little deeper, to make absolutely sure that all the 'i's have been dotted and all the 't's crossed. Unfortunately, however, it all too frequently turns out to be the loose thread on a favourite jumper which, when pulled, unravels the whole thing. Perhaps a new person has seen the idea for the first time and feels the need to go through the whole process of understanding how it came about, and how it is to be rationalized, and an issue that was resolved is suddenly thrown into debate again. Or perhaps time is short, and 'Just a couple of groups' becomes an eight-week hiatus which creates the need for all sorts of corners to be cut at critical stages further down the track – flavour refinement, packaging development, etc. – which can seriously endanger product delivery.

Let's go back to our banana yoghurts for an example.

The Yoghurt Files

Banana yoghurt concept

Insight: We all love bananas and know that they're full of healthy energy. But we don't think to eat them very often.

Proposition: Fresh banana yoghurt. All the healthy goodness and slow release energy of fresh Caribbean bananas with delicious natural yoghurt provides a sweet but good for you snack that keeps you going.

Team question: Let's just check whether it has to be Caribbean bananas?

Group feedback: "I don't really like bananas"
"I don't need extra energy"
"I didn't know bananas came from the Caribbean"

Banana yoghurt concept – revised

Insight: Bananas are very healthy so we should eat more of them

Proposition: Fresh yoghurt with banana. All the vitamins, minerals and carbohydrates of bananas with delicious natural yoghurt that gives you a great snack any time

---

Team question: Let's just check other fruits apart from banana again...

Group feedback: "I like strawberries"
"I prefer raspberries"
"Mandarins are my favourite"
"Aren't blueberries a super food?"

> ## Banana yoghurt concept – re-revised
>
> *Insight:*   Fruit is healthy
>
> *Proposition:*   Fruit yoghurts for all the family

Avoidance strategies

- *Stick to your plan*: Decide at the outset how many rounds of testing you will do and stick to it! (easy to say – tough to do).
- *Just say "no"*: Once the idea is born and has a life of its own, don't weigh it down with ever more tests. Trust your judgement and let it fly.

No. 5: Killing by proxy

Ah, the tyranny of invisible decisions (and faceless decision makers!)! How many times have we sat in meetings to review initial ideas only to find ideas being herded off the desk and into the bin like plague carriers because 'the boss wouldn't like it'. If bosses only knew how many ideas were ditched before they even reached their ears because they felt like, seemed like, or were even just vaguely a little bit like something that once in a previous era had been fiercely rejected. It seems that bosses are never allowed to change their minds (shows weakness) or to have more than one point of view (shows indecision) even from one project or brand to another. If you profess not to be a fan of a kids version of product X, then for all time no kids concepts will ever reach your desk. This is 'killing by proxy'.

It is a particularly harsh and effective killer because it arrives so early in the ideation process – that is to say, at birth. In workshops, if you choose a team all well acquainted with their boss they will even edit out ideas by proxy before they open their mouths, often subconsciously. The 'Boss Filter' is firmly in place from the get-go. Of course it's not just

---

Box 12.1: Killing by proxy

Simpkins:	Right chaps, I think we've cracked it. Banana yoghurt – but premium, made with real banana pieces.
Jones:	Can't do it, the boss wouldn't like a yellow fruit concept.
Smith:	We've tried yellow before.
Jones:	Hates yellow.
Simpkins:	Alright then, guava. Something a bit different.
Smith:	Won't work. Consumers wouldn't like it. They just like what they're used to.
Jones:	Like strawberries.
Smith:	Love strawberries.
Simpkins:	Strawberries then. But premium. Lots of real fruit.
Jones:	Won't wash with R&D – they'd never get it done for the money.
Smith:	Just not set up for that sort of thing.
Simpkins:	Fewer pieces? But chunky so you can really taste the fruit?
Smith:	You're forgetting our competitors. That's exactly what they'd expect us to do and they'd kill us.
Jones:	Absolutely. We'd never get away with it with them in the market.
Simpkins:	So what we're saying is we should produce a fairly fruity, non-premium, strawberry yoghurt.
Smith & Jones:	That's it!
Simpkins:	Ah.

---

bosses who play higher authority here – killing by proxy (Box 12.1) can be done in the name of a great many things.

Avoidance strategies

- *Use naïve resources*: Involve people new to your team and the category, but smart in other ways, in your brainstorming sessions to get round the 'edit before you speak' issue.
- *Don't take it for granted*: Make sure you don't' take killing-by-proxy statements for granted. Retort with "have you asked him/her?" when a proxy argument is made. And then don't accept the reply "there is no need to, I already know what the answer would be. . .". Always ask.

- *Let consumers be the judge*: If the proxy is a competitor, the stock response needs to become "let's see what consumers think about that" and take it from there.

No. 6: The off-guard boss

Subtly different to killing by proxy this is another all time killer. The idea in question is not rejected at source by proxy (hooray!) but instead is subjected to the fiery furnace of the off-guard boss (damn and blast!). The off-guard bosses can best be identified by the distant look fixed in their eyes and the furrowed brow of someone whose current worry will be their only focus until solved. They lurk in corridors and canteens all around the world and move at a pace all their own. These are the 'bosses in the middle of a crisis'. This crisis exists in their own area and is usually brought on by a seemingly random call from someone on the board asking for figures or analysis on something they didn't even know existed or at the very least didn't know was their responsibility (often because it wasn't prior to the phone call). "Do you have the figures for our retailer margins across the world, by SKU split by larger than 1 litre and smaller than 250 ml... I need them by lunch." Or even "What's our strategy with this new competitor X?... Well, you're the Marketing Director! I want it on my desk by 8 am – I'm spending tomorrow morning letting the Chairman beat me at golf." And then, in the midst of this deluge of high stress from high places, up pops the Marketing Manager enthusiastically waving a piece of paper. This is most likely to take place in the canteen queue, or as an ambush in the corridor between the toilet and the Director's office – places where there is no escaping the impromptu approach. Not wanting to waste any of the Director's time the manager précis his intro and gets straight to the point – as in Box 12.2.

What do we think will be produced for him on the morn? Exactly – several twists on his strawberry idea (strawberry yoghurt with Hampshire strawberries, strawberry yoghurt with Israeli strawberries, strawberry yoghurt with no strawberries) and not a single banana version in sight. In a single 10-second interchange the whole project has been derailed and the banana version, born of real insight, has been ditched. Is it the Director's fault? The Marketing Manager's? It's neither, really – it was inevitable. Uninformed, off-guard and

Box 12.2: The off-guard boss	
Simpkins:	Ah, glad I've caught you
MD:	Not now Simpkins
Simpkins:	This won't take a mo – just need to get your thoughts before we commit to this
MD:	Not a good time Simpkins
Simpkins:	It's the Project Spectrum concepts
MD:	Look, I really don't have...
Simpkins:	Banana! That's the big new idea. We do it with bananas!
MD:	Bananas?
Simpkins:	We're calling them 'Schneubels'
MD:	What are you talking about?
Simpkins:	'Banana Schneubels for all the family'
MD:	Bananas? I thought we said strawberries? Everyone likes strawberries
Simpkins:	Yes, but we thought...
MD:	Pull yourself together Simpkins. Now just get on with it and bring me some good ideas tomorrow

stressed the Director has simply given clear input to his underling in where to direct the innovation project. So it's just a result of poor planning, and a misunderstanding of the nature of ideas and how protected they must be. To avoid a tragedy, think comedy. It's all in the timing.

Avoidance strategies

- *Plan in a quickie*: If you have to do regular updates with your senior manager, plan them in. Ten minutes immediately after a brainstorm session will do, if it's in their diary and is being guarded by a PA, the reception will be less hostile and the views more balanced. Remember the 7 p's: 'Proper Planning and Preparation Prevents Piss Poor Performance.' Choose your moment wisely.
- *Stay regular*: If possible don't update senior managers too often. Their desire to keep on top of the process might kill valuable ideas. Plan in and stick to review sessions at appropriate times. Well-briefed directors reviewing well-presented ideas gives even the wackiest suggestion a chance of surviving and bringing value at a later stage.

No. 7: 'Yes, but. . .'

The old dame of innovation killers. It's been around a long time and is well known to all, but persistent as ever, it is the ivy of the marketing garden – even when you kill it off it just keeps coming back, stronger than ever (Figure 12.5). An old dame called Ivy, then. In a market garden. Sort of.

The 'yes, but'-er loves a good meeting. One where issues are flying back and forth and enthusiasm for new ideas is rife – the perfect breeding ground for the introduction of their trademark comments: "Yes, but it will be too expensive/too big/too small/too late. . ." The truth is that it just might be too good an opportunity to miss, but let the 'yes, but'-ers run free and you'll never know. As Peter Drucker said 'Beware the "Yes, but"-ers. Always full of comment and points of view, right up until they "Yes, but" you right out of business.' The only thing more damaging in this arena is the 'yes, but'-er's sardonic cousin, the 'no,but'-er. These are the "It'll never work and it's a rubbish idea anyway" brigade, bereft of the necessary enthusiasm to even want the ideas to work and devoid of decent suggestions with which to replace them. Dangerous even in small numbers, beware of the 'no, but'-er (except for diet products).

Figure 12.5: Yes-butter.

Avoidance strategies

- *Swear box*: Put a money box in each of your meeting rooms. Every time someone says 'Yes, but' they have to put in a coin. Give the proceeds to a local worthy cause or to the summer party bar bill fund (a worthy cause at your local).
- *'Yes, and...'*: Train yourselves to think and say 'Yes, and...'. In other words, to make every comment an opportunity for adding value and finding ways of making something work better. It is simply amazing what can be achieved by this kind of small redirection in energy at this early stage in the idea creation process. Even if your natural inclination is to say "yes, but" to an idea, force yourself to replace it with "yes, and". In other words, ditch the negativity, and don't just sit there quietly saying nothing because you want to point out a potential shortcoming but know you shouldn't – force yourself to speak up and to come up with a suitable build, even if it seems like an implausible idea.

No. 8: Poor casting

Casting isn't just for the movies (see Figure 12.6). Who you have in your innovation team is just as important as what they do. And don't just look for brilliant individuals – look for the right mix to make a brilliant team. Ideally you want people who spark off each other, get each other fired up – even if it's slightly antagonistic. Devil's advocates can give the team something to push against, and sometimes a little tension can go a long way to delivering great ideas. Even out and out mavericks have a role here. They can be the grit that makes the oyster in the team, from which is born the pearl of a great idea.

Appointing the right person to run your innovation project is obviously crucial to its success, but the selection can be difficult. To make it simpler, remember that there are basically two types of project leader:

1 *The spark*: The young gun who is always fizzing with new ideas. It's great to make sparks responsible for an innovation project as their enthusiasm will be infectious, and they are almost guaranteed to generate loads of ideas. But they may well be the type who are continually coming up with more and more new ideas, and find it hard to spot the single

Figure 12.6: Mission Innovation III – a well-cast film.

'big idea', and have difficulty focusing on it once it has been identified. Almost certainly they will not be the right people to lead the team in choosing and then crafting the final concept.

2 *The multi-tasker*: This person is very buttoned down, organized, thorough and capable of juggling all the balls that are thrown in during an innovation project. The issue here is that even the most diligent workers, if they don't have a love of ideas and if they don't really feel comfortable with the new and different, can kill ideas more effectively than almost anything else.

Avoidance strategies

- *Opposites Attract*: Always have a team of opposites on an innovation project. Ideally including a spark and a multi-tasker. You have to cast for the sparks that fly, as well as for the efficiency of the process.
- *Use your briefs*: Write yourself a casting brief for each member of the team. It doesn't have to be long and detailed, just a few lines will do. Then see if you can cast as close as possible to the roles you have outlined.

No. 9: Giving up

It's sad but true – sometimes teams simply don't believe an innovation can be solved and just give up. In its mildest guise this usually takes the form of settling; teams settle for the best they have rather than the best they could make it. This is often the result of a protracted concept test phase. Endless rounds of testing with consumers will dull enthusiasm for the quest for perfection. This was something of which Henry Royce, the brilliant engineer of Rolls-Royce Motor Cars fame, was well aware. He always insisted that his teams "Accept nothing that is nearly right or good enough", telling them instead to "Find the best that exists and make it better. If it does not exist, invent it." In more severe cases teams simply abandon a troublesome innovation altogether. The most likely time for this to happen is after the first concept test where all the team's hopes rest on that great idea they put in. It bombs with consumers and their hopes are dashed, enthusiasm disappears amid quiet thoughts of wondering why they bothered in the first place, and the project is abandoned. This attitude is understandable, of course, but you need to develop a mindset among your team akin to that of the great innovators who understand that failure is but fuel on the fire of their eventual success.

Never stop

The most amazing thing about James Dyson, the inventor of the Dual-Cyclone vacuum cleaner, is not that his invention was rejected by all the major players before he went off and did it himself, nor is it that his Dyson DC range went from first launch to brand leader in both upright and cylinder vacuum cleaners in the UK in just three years, beating the venerable Hoover and a host of others. No, it is the fact that, when you see his first working prototype, it is numbered 5127. That means there were 5126 prototypes before it which didn't work. Give up? He clearly doesn't know the meaning of the words (see Figure 12.7). As he told *Ingenia* in September 2005: 'If I had listened to those who could only shed doom and gloom on my idea, then it would have been quashed very early on. As an innovator you must have obdurate faith in your idea.'

Avoidance strategies

- *Do a Dyson*: Have faith, persevere and focus on fixing any problems. Trust in your own ingenuity more than the nay-sayers and doom mongers. Take consumer feedback

Early prototypes   Final prototypes No.5127   Dyson DC01

Figure 12.7: The development of the Dyson Dual-Cyclone vacuum cleaner.

as stimulus for finding new solutions. Understand that each set back is only a potential building block for something even better.

- *Create your own kind of test*: Use prototypes as much as possible, no matter how basic. We all know that 80% of communication is non-verbal, yet we still persist in using written concepts to present our ideas. Why? Buck the trend and design a test that looks at your idea the way you see it.

 ## Handover

We have now come to the end of *Return on Ideas*. I hope the idea of Rocketing has stimulated you to look again at your innovation process, and has given you some practical real-world methods in which to change the way you develop ideas and run projects. With a little luck you may be at the start of getting more from all the energy, time and resource you put into creating new ideas for your brands. Whatever you are attempting to innovate, I wish you luck.

Rocketing toolkit

APPENDIX

Item	Title	Chapter
Figure 4.7	The innovation timesheet	Innovation isn't working
Table 6.1	Factors influencing innovation process design	Rocketing: Destination
Box 6.3	Quick Innovation Brief	Rocketing: Destination
Figure 7.5	R&D treasure hunt briefing proforma	Rocketing: Combustion
Table 7.1	360° Insight checklist	Rocketing: Combustion
Table 7.2	Different types of brainstorming session	Rocketing: Combustion
Table 7.3	10 Brainstorming techniques anyone can do	Rocketing: Combustion
Box 8.1	Summary of Theatre Rules	Rocketing: Nozzle
Table 8.1	Idea Power criteria	Rocketing: Nozzle
Table 9.1	360° Mix checklist	Rocketing: Expander
Table 12.1	Nine innovation pitfalls	Avoiding the pitfalls

	Days
1. Generating and crafting ideas	☐
2. Evaluating and testing ideas	☐
3. Writing justifications	☐
4. Presenting ideas 'for info' to committees/other departments	☐
Total creativity (1)	☐
Total Admin (2 + 3 + 4)	☐
Ratio	―

Figure 4.7: The innovation timesheet.

Table 6.1: Factors influencing process design.

Speed is paramount	SPEED	More relaxed timelines
• Process steps in parallel • Real time inputs from experts in workshops • Longer workshops with evening consumer input • On the spot design		• Inputs from multiple sources; experts from all markets • Multiple shorter workshops with time to 'noodle' in between • Use a design agency to add real thought & value
Tight Focus	BANDWIDTH	**Broad scope**
• Fresh, diverse inputs • Different teams approaching the same problem • Express ideas in different formats: drawings, longhand descriptions, etc.		• Get insight and inputs across the full spectrum • Divide areas up amongst the team • Build in moments when focus is narrowed and choices are made
Senior stakeholders	WHO'S INVOLVED	**Regional/local teams**
• Hold separate brainstorming sessions for senior input • Do regular one-on-one feedback sessions • Capture senior comments in an Idea Power matrix – not in front of the whole team		• Parallel brainstorming sessions in each local market, then pooling ideas • Update calls to local markets after significant workshops • Put key dates in diaries at the start – then have an open invitation
Concept test	MILESTONE FORMAT	**Big presentation**
• Plan a quick and dirty online test before full test • Brief copywriters to perfect your ideas in real consumer speak		• Brief agencies to create 3D mock-ups and 'stuff' • Plan in time to rehearse

Box 6.3: Quick Innovation Brief

Innovation Vision: _____

Business Objective: _____

Brand Idea: _____

Target: _____

Source of Gains: _____

'Drop-Dead' lines: _____

Senior Experts: _____

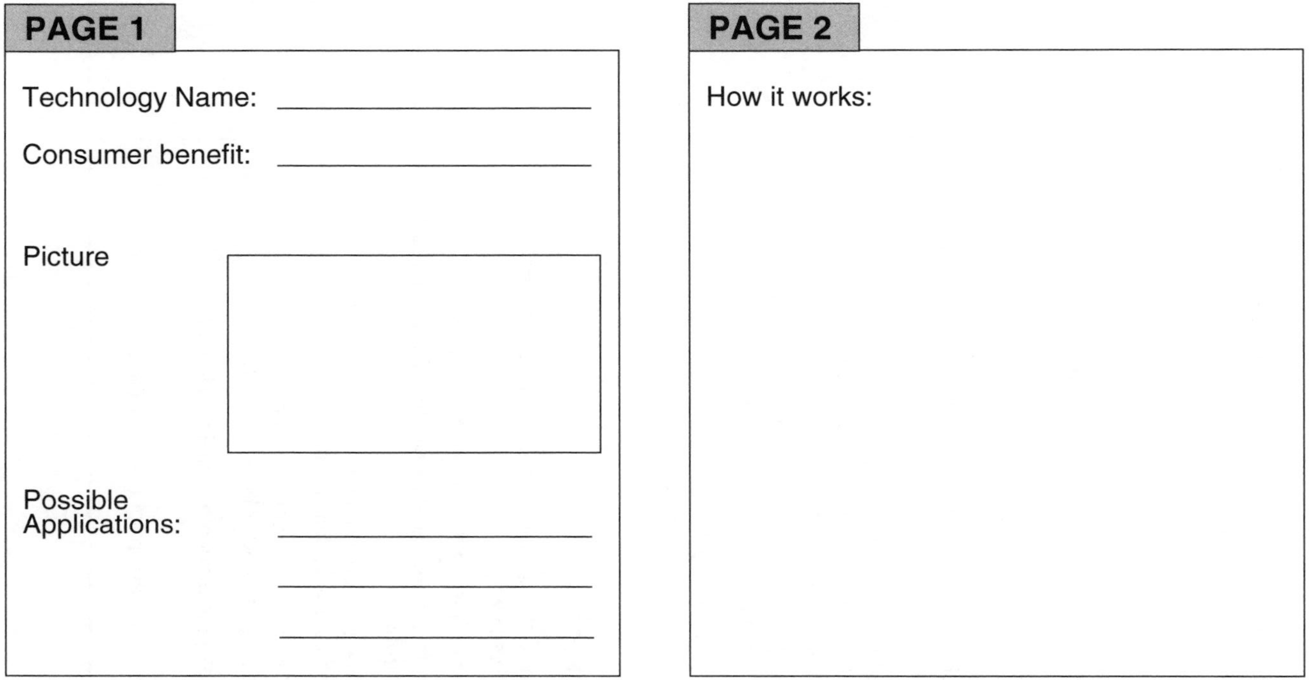

PAGE 2

How it works:

PAGE 1

Technology Name:

Consumer benefit:

Picture

Possible
Applications:

Figure 7.5: R&D treasure hunt briefing proforma.

Table 7.1: 360° insight checklist.

Insight Source	Description	Timing	Resp.	$
Observation	• Go to where consumers consume/use your product and just watch			
Fringe consumers	• Interview people you've never talked to before, at the (scary) fringes			
Semiotics	• Look at the body language of your brand and category. Use expert Semioticians			
Trends	• Look at what is changing in culture and society. Get fresh trends each year			
Experts	• Talk to experts in your category; media pundits, consultants, academics, etc.			
Competitive landscaping	• Gather competitive products from all adjacent categories and rethink your market. Do this globally if relevant			
R&D treasure hunt	• Get R&D to show you what they've got in their cupboard early on. It's surprising			
Global Category Trawl	• Look for weird and wonderful stuff from emergent markets like Japan. Go broad			
Copy & roll out	• Look at what is successful in other markets in your category. Copy it			
Emerging passions	• Get in the know on what is cool and emergent. Ask yourself why . . .			
Retail Visits	• Put yourself in the shoes of the retailer • Go to a store and experience the buying 'moment of truth'			
Competences	• What are your company's competences? • Look across other business units			
Competences	• What are your company's competences? • Look across other business units			
Qualitative research	• Make the feedback visual and interactive			
Quantitative research	• Focus on the insight not just the data			

Table 7.2: Different type of brainstorming session.

Type	Objective	Techniques to try	Location and style
Focused	• To generate ideas for a specific target, need and for occasion in a particular category with a known product type	• Role play • Heaven and hell • Random word game	• On or off site • Half to full day • High energy from the start
Blue sky	• To generate ideas across a broad spectrum of categories with any number of possible products	• Break category rules • Corporation takeover • Film start takeover	• Off-site • Full day for 3 days • Take time needed to get out of 'normal business' mode
Insight platform	• To generate ideas against a set of defined consumer insights	• Cross referencing • Role play • Consumer immersion	• Off site in a consumer space (bar, home etc.) • Full day for 2 days • Get immersed in consumer world
Quickie	• To generate ideas quickly stimulated by a specific fresh input	• Yes, and … • Colours/music • Trend extrapolation	• On site/wherever you are • 40 mins to 2 hrs + • High energy • Small group (2–5)

●━━━━━━━●

NB. Any technique can be used in any session

Table 7.3: 10 brainstorming techniques anyone can do.

	Technique	Description	Time to do
1.	Heaven and hell	• Write the worst of all possible innovations (Hell) • Turn each into a practical positive idea (Heaven)	30 mins
2.	Role play	• Create a picture & pen portrait of your consumer • Role play it back to the group as idea stimulus	45 mins 45 mins
3.	Random word game	• 2–4 people do random word association in turn • Rest of team listen and generate ideas	15 mins
4.	Break category rules	• List all spoken & unspoken rules of your category • Break each rule to create a new idea	30 mins 30 mins
5.	(a) Corporate takeover	• List key success factors of a big successful brand • Imagine their management team takes over	30 mins
	(b) Personality takeover	• List the key qualities of a well known personality	30 mins
6.	Cross referencing	• Populate 2 axes with key aspects of your brand • Force connections between all to find new ideas	45 mins
7.	Consumer immersion	• Go to a consumer hang out; bar, home, shop . . . • Watch, listen & learn then create ideas	60 mins
8.	Yes, and . . .	• Build on others ideas instantly by reacting with 'Yes, and (my idea)'.	5 mins
9.	Colours/Music	• Write down all associations to music or a colour • Use associations to create new ideas	15 mins
10.	Trends extrapolation	• Take a trend and image it dominates culture • Turn implications into ideas for your brand	30 mins

Box 8.1: Summary of Theatre Rules

Prototype	Draw a picture, make a mock-up, use imagery. Pictures communicate faster than words. Use them.
Set the scene	Get the right ambience for presenting ideas. Go to a coffee shop. Change the lighting. Mood matters.
Use props	Bring examples from other categories. Show what others have achieved to enhance your ideas.
Tell a story	Warm them up. Draw them in. This is innovation foreplay.
Rehearse	Try it all out. Get some feedback. Learn your opening line.

Table 8.1: Idea Power criteria.

Criteria	Explanation	Scoring
Fit to brand	Does it deliver on your brand vision?	Hi, Med, Lo
Consumer appeal	Do consumers love it?	Hi, Med, Lo
Relevant differentiation	How different & better do consumers see it vs competition?	Hi, Med, Lo
Feasibility	How easy is it to do?	Easy, Hard, Very hard
Expertise required	Does your business have the skills to deliver this idea	In team, In company, Buy in
Investment	How much would it cost to be able to make this?	Hi, Med, Lo
Global applicability	How many markets is this applicable to?	Local only, A few, Most
Margin	How much money will this generate for us, per unit?	Hi, Med, Lo
Passion	How excited are you by this idea?	Hi, Med, Lo

Table 9.1: 360° Mix checklist.

Element	Challenge	Action
Product Benefit	• Is your new benefit consumer perceivable? • Are you different enough from competitors? • What is new/emerging – are you leading?	

Product Format	• Are you unique enough across:
	  – Shape
	  – Smell
	  – Colour
	  – Texture
	  – In use characteristics (e.g. pouring)
	• Portion size: how can you be more relevant?	

Pack Design	• How can you stand out…
	  – vs. competitors
	  – Across markets
	  – With best in class	

Consumer Communications	• Who's cutting through? How can you? • Are you getting the most you can out of new media? • What media assets can you create?	
Intermediary/ Professional Communications	• How can you be recommended more? • What value can you bring to intermediaries' lives/jobs? • What other brands have relationships you could piggyback?	
In-Store	• What are the retailer's objectives – can you work with them? • Are you considering secondary siting? • Who is cutting through in store? What can you learn/steal? • How can your secondary packaging bring a benefit to the retailer or consumer?	
New Channels	• What other channels are your competitors in? • What new channels are emerging? • What new channels could you create?	
Pack Structure	• How can you add a benefit with the pack? • Are you unique enough in shape and substrate? • How can you improve your closure? • How can you improve home storage? • What about disposability, recycling?	
Pricing	• Are new approaches being used? • What can you steal from other categories (e.g. Mobile phones)?	

Table 12.1: Nine innovation pitfalls.

Pitfall	Avoidance Strategy
1. Oops, the product is useless	• Clear, consumer relevant action standards • Get R&D involved right from the start • Prototype early • Try the product out with real people early on
2. 'Not invented here' syndrome	• Evaluate using Idea Power matrices, for objectivity • Reward people for bringing ideas from outside • Rewrite other's ideas in your own style before using them
3. The 'could it be' killer	• Stick to your original vision • Credit the team with ideas, not individuals
4. Over-testing	• Stick to your plan • Just say 'no'
5. Killing by proxy	• Use naïve resources • Don't take it for granted, challenge the killer-by-proxy • Let consumers be the judge
6. The off-guard boss	• Plan in a quickie, don't take them by surprise • Stay regular, keep to your review timings
7. 'Yes, but'-ters	• Install a 'Yes, but...' swear box in your meeting rooms • Use 'Yes, and..' as a permanent replacement
8. Poor casting	• Write briefs for each innovation role and cast to them • Build a team for the quantity of sparks that fly
9. Giving up	• Do a Dyson – have faith, persevere and never give up • Create your own kind of test

Index

3 bucket principle   64,
    128–33, 214
3 mobile phones   176–7
3M   37, 134, 160–1, 164
15 % rule, 3M   134
360° insight   96–109
Actimel, Danone   183–5
Adcept concepts   126–7
Added Value   98, 130, 147,
    149
administration   33, 36
agencies   217–18
Aloe Vera products   105
ambience, location   145–6,
    251
American Express   183,
    192–3
Apollo spacecraft   59–60
Apple   34–5, 79, 88–91,
    114–15
Armstrong, Neil   59

Bacardi Breezer   172–3
banana yoghurt example
    227–8, 230, 232–3
bandwidth of ideas   75–6,
    245
'beige' innovations   225
Ben & Jerry's ice cream   132
Bertolli   117
Best of Both bread   183,
    188–9
Blackberry mobile email   27
blandness   88

Bliss drinks   116–17
Blue Ocean Strategy (Chan
    Kim & Mauborgne)
    33, 47
Blue Sky brainstorming
    116–17, 249
Boo.com   224
books, business   7–9
Brainchild protest group   43
brainstorming   94, 110–27,
    249–50
    Apple Macintosh/Lisa
      114–15
    Brainstorming from Hell
      123
    concept types   124–7
    Idea Power matrices
      155–6
    parallel sessions   110–15
    session types   115–18,
      135, 249
    ten techniques   118–23,
      249
    uninspiring sessions   123
    see also 'combustion'
      ideas generation
The Brand Gym books
    (Taylor)   8, 70
brands   70–2, 151–2,
    181–203, 252
briefs   83–7, 240, 246
building ideas   162–9
    being nice   164–9
    combining ideas   162–3

positive attitudes   163–4,
    166
research   167–9
senior executives   165–9
winning ideas   157
see also 'expander'
    development stage
business books   7–9

Calippo Shots   13–21, 103
    ice balls   18
    ideas generation   16–18
    launching   20
    market growth   14
    packaging   19–20
    refreshment vision   14
    Solero Shots   20
    success factors   16,
      18–20
    teenage market   14–17,
      20
    ten top ideas   18–19
    winning mixes   19–20
canned soft drinks   14–17
casting, teams   238–40, 254
category rule-breaking
    119–20, 250
CEOs *see* chief executive
    officers
Chan Kim, W.   33, 47
change, resistance to
    160–1, 165
chief executive officers
    (CEOs)

chief executive officers
    (CEOs)   (cont.)
  innovation   25, 51–2
  Jobs of Apple   79, 88–91
  McKnight of 3M   37
child development   70–2
chilled foods   209
Christensen, Clayton M.   33
clear vision   62–3, 69, 77–8
  see also 'destination'
    envisioning
Coca-Cola   80–1, 118
Coco Pops, Kellogg   32
colours, brainstorming   119,
    122, 250
combustion chambers,
    rockets   61
'combustion' ideas
    generation   62–4,
    93–137
  brainstorming   110–27
  checklist   137
  insight   63, 95–109
  quality of ideas   93–4
  three bucket principle
    64, 128–33
  year overview   134–6
communications   171, 253
competences   107–8, 248
competitive landscaping
    102–3, 248
concept tests   75, 77, 157,
    245
constructive thinking   32
consumers
  avoiding pitfalls   225–6,
    235
  brainstorming   119, 121,
    250
  feedback   152
  insight   98–9, 216–17,
    248

new products   170
observation   119, 121
product appeal   151–2,
    252
Project Blues   216–17
research   95, 150, 152,
    155
cooking presentation   146
Cooper, Robert   30
copying   105–6, 248
core business innovation
    47–52
Core concepts   124–5
Core Design   174
'corporate takeover'
    brainstorming
    119–20, 250
costs   38–40
'could it be...' pitfall
    229–31, 254
creativity   79, 214–15
cross referencing   119,
    121–2, 250
cultural aspects   106–7

Danone   183–5
databases   133
deadlines   78–81
decision-making   79–80,
    210–13, 233–5
deconstructive thinking   32
design agencies   217–18
designing the process   63,
    74–7, 245
  breadth of ideas   75–6
  influential factors   75–7
  milestones enroute   75,
    77
  project teams   75–7
  time frames   75
destination, rockets   60–1

'destination' envisioning
    62–3, 69–92, 246
  brand usage   70–2
  clear vision   62–3, 69
  deadlines   78–81
  designing the process
    63, 74–7
  hamster-wheeling   73
  keeping end in mind   63,
    74–81
  market segmentation
    81–4
  vision painting   87–91
Detailed concepts   127
developing ideas see
    'expander'
    development stage
differentiation of ideas   152,
    252
digestive medicines   107
Dragon's Den TV series   142
'drop-dead' lines   78–81, 86
Drucker, Peter   237
Dual-Cyclone vacuum
    cleaner   241
Dyson, James   241–2

egg online services   146–7
email   27
European soft drinks market
    82–3
evaluating ideas   64, 150–1,
    161–2
  see also 'nozzle' screening
'expander' development
    stage   62, 64–5,
    159–78, 253
  building ideas   162–9
  checklists   171, 177, 253
  executing ideas   170
  feedback   170–6

launching ideas   172,
   176–7
resistance to change
   160–1, 165
senior expertise   65
experimental doodling   37
expertise
   Innovation Funnel   36–7
   insight   101–2, 248
   required by idea   153,
      252
   senior   65, 75–6, 86
external creatives   214–15

facilitators   115
failure   28–9, 42, 173
feasibility of ideas   153, 252
feedback   152, 170–6
fifteen percent rule, 3M   134
Focused brainstorming
   116–17, 249
Frigo (Unilever Spain)   14,
   18
Frubes, Yoplait   183, 198–9
Fry, Art   161

G4, Apple   88
Gillette   49–51
Gizmondo   225
global/local pitfalls   227–8
global markets   154, 252
global research   105, 248
Google   173
'grave-robbing' old ideas
   131–3
Gü   182–3, 200–1

Hargadon, Andrew   131–2
'heaven and hell'
   brainstorming
   118–19, 250

Hero   175–6
Hillis, Danny   110
Holiday Skin body lotion
   183, 196–7
Hovis   183, 188–9
Hutchinson Telecom   176

iBook, Apple   88
ice cream business   13–21,
   98, 103, 106, 144
Idea Amnesty sessions   135
Idea Power   142, 150–7,
   252
   avoiding pitfalls   228
   benefits   156
   concept tests   157
   criteria   151–4, 252
   matrices   151, 154–5
   winning ideas   157
Idea Sketch concepts   124
ideas generation   16–18,
   214–15
   see also 'combustion'
      ideas generation
ideation see ideas generation
iMac, Apple   88
impact of ideas   65–6
ingenuity   79
innovation   25–54
   Calippo Shots   13–21
   core business   47–52
   Innovation Funnel   1–2,
      25, 29–47, 52, 53
   overview   1–3
   pitfalls   221–42
   radical innovation   47–52
   'rebellion' process   2, 25,
      51–2
   Rocketing approach
      2–3, 57–178, 243–54
   speed of process
      207–19, 245

ten successes   181–203
Innovation Funnel   1–2, 25,
   29–47, 52
   administration   33, 36
   Apple iPods   34–5
   costs   38–40
   death spiral   46–7
   deconstructive thinking
      32
   expertise focus   36–7
   insight   44
   marketing   45–6
   picking winners   32
   proprietary components
      34–5
   quality of ideas   40–2
   Sony Walkman   34–5
   stage-gate system   30–2,
      53, 139
   stifling innovation
      32–46, 53
   time concerns   36
   wastage of ideas   42–3
insight   63, 95–109, 248
   checklists   96–7, 108–9,
      248
   coffee breaks   107–8
   competences   107–8
   competitive landscaping
      102–3
   consumers   98–9,
      216–17
   copying   105–6
   definition   96
   emerging passions
      106–7
   experts   101–2
   global research   105
   ideas generation   16–17
   Innovation Funnel   44
   new technologies   103–4
   observation   98

insight   *(cont.)*
    Pampers   71
    research   95, 97–8
    semiotics   99–100
    shopping   107
    speed of process
        216–17
    360 ° insight   96–109,
        248
    trends   100–1
Insight Platform
    brainstorming
    116–17, 249
international teams   76
intranets   133
investment   153, 252
iPod, Apple   34–5

Jobs, Steve   79, 88–91
Johnson's   183, 196–7

Kandoo toilet wipes   72
Kellogg's Coco Pops   32
'killing by proxy' pitfalls
    233–5, 254
Klarke, Kimberly   99
Knorr Vie shots   84
Kotex sanitary products   99
Kraft   49

lead markets   175–6
leadership types   238–9
limited distribution launches
    172
Lisa, Apple   90, 114–15
Live Aid   141
local/global pitfalls   227–8
location ambience   145–6,
    251
L'Oréal   170

Mac World Expo   79
Macintosh, Apple   88–91,
    114–15
McKinsey consultants   133
McKnight, William L.   37
Magnum ice cream   106
management, senior
    165–9, 211–12, 233–6
*Managing Creativity and
    Innovation* (Harvard
    Business Essentials)
    31
managing ideas *see* three
    bucket principle
Managing Innovation (Tidd
    et al)   30
map of the book   6
margins   154, 252
markets
    ice cream   14
    Innovation Funnel   45–6
    lead markets   175–6
    research   95, 150
    segmentation   81–4
    soft drinks   14–17, 82–3
Mates Rates, T-Mobile   183,
    186–7
matrices, Idea Power   151,
    154–5
Mauborgne, Rénee   33, 47
Mayer, Marissa   173
mix *see* winning mixes
Moore's Law   110–11
Motorola   183, 190–1
multi-parallel idea sessions
    214–15
multi-tasker team leader
    240
multiple brainstorming
    110–15
music   119, 122, 145, 250

needs-based segmentation
    7–9
Newton's third law of
    motion   60
nice, being nice   164–9
'not invented here'
    syndrome   226–9, 254
'nozzle' screening   62, 64,
    139–58
    checklist   157
    evaluating ideas   64
    external screening
        150–7
    Idea Power   142, 150–7,
        252
    internal screening   143–9
    prioritizing ideas   64
    showbusiness approach
        64, 140–57
nozzles, rockets   61
NRMA car breakdown
    service   97

Oat So Simple, Quaker
    49–50
observation   98, 119, 121,
    248
Ocado   182–3, 202–3
OMO detergent   148
Owen Jones, Lyndsay   170

packaging   19–20, 39, 171,
    253
Pampers   70–2
parallel brainstorming
    sessions   110–15,
    214–15
passions   106–7, 154, 248,
    252
Pedigree Pet Foods   127,
    131

Peperami 173–5
performing ideas 64,
142–9, 251
'personality takeover'
brainstorming
119–21, 250
Petit Filous Frubes 183,
198–9
pitfalls 221–42, 254
avoidance 221–42
'beige' innovations 225
'could it be...' 229–31
decisions by proxy
233–5
giving up 240–1
global/local problems
227–8
invisible pitfalls 223
'killing by proxy' 233–5
nine pitfalls 223–41
nondescript products
225
'not invented here'
syndrome 226–9
the off-guard boss
235–6
over-testing 231–3
poor team casting
238–40
recognising pitfalls 222
too many refinements
229–31
under-resourced
improvements 224–6
unfulfilled claims 223–6
useless products 223–6
'Yes, but...' comments
237–8
positive attitudes 163–4,
166
Post-Its 161
Powerade 80–1, 118

PowerPoint 140, 142–3,
147
presentations 75, 77,
143–9, 245
see also theatre rules
pricing systems 171, 253
prioritization 64, 79
see also 'nozzle' screening
Procter & Gamble 163
Project Blues 209–10,
212–18
proprietary components
34–5
props in presentations
146–7, 251
prototypes 145, 226,
240–1, 251

Quaker Oat So Simple
49–50
qualitative research 97, 248
quality of ideas 40–2, 93–4
quantitative research 97–8,
150, 248
Quick Innovation Brief 246
Quickie brainstorming
sessions 116–18, 135,
249

R&D see research &
development team
radical innovation 47–52
random word games
119–20, 250
Raskin, Jeff 89
razors, Gillette 49–51
RAZR phone, Motorola
183, 190–1
reading business books
5–9

'rebellion' innovation
process 2, 25, 51–2
Red card, American Express
183, 192–3
refining ideas 229–31
rehearsing 148–9, 251
relevant differentiation 152,
252
Renault Scenic car 183,
194–5
research
building ideas 167–9
consumers 95, 150, 152,
156
insight 95, 97–8, 103–5,
248
marketing 95
research & development
(R&D) team 103–4,
226, 247–8
Research in Motion (RIM)
27
retail visits 107, 248
RIM see Research in Motion
risk of bad ideas 113
rocket motors 57–62
Rocketing innovation
approach 2–3,
57–178, 243–54
'combustion' ideas
generation 62–4,
93–137
'destination' envisioning
62–3, 69–92, 246
'expander' development
stage 62, 64–5,
159–78, 253
the motor 62–7
'nozzle' screening 62,
64, 139–58
toolkit 243–54
role play 119, 250

Rolls-Royce Motor Cars   240
Royce, Henry   240

Saturn rockets   59–60
scenario modelling   156
scene-setting   145–6, 251
scoring, Idea Power   151,
    154–5
Scotchguard   164
Scottish Courage   116–17
screening ideas *see* 'nozzle'
    screening
segmentation   7–9, 81–4
semiotics   99–100, 248
senior expertise   36–7, 65,
    75–6, 86
senior management   165–9,
    211–12, 233–6
shopping   107, 248
showbusiness approach
    140–57
  Idea Power   142, 150–7,
    252
  performing ideas   64,
    142–9, 251
  theatre rules   64, 142–9,
    251
Simulated Test Market (STM)
    170, 172
skunk working   66
smoothies   84
soft drinks market   14–17,
    82–3
Solero Shots   20
Sony Walkman   34–5
Southcorp wine exporter
    98
'spark' team leader   238–9
speed of process   207–19,
    245
  agencies   217–18
  checklists   218–19

decision-making   210–13
insight   216–17
parallel brainstorming
    214–15
principles   209–10
Project Blues   209–10,
    212–18
small teams   212–14
stage-gate system   30–2, 53,
    139
stakeholders   75–8, 155,
    213, 245
STM *see* Simulated Test
    Market
story-telling   147–8, 251
Streets ice cream   144
Sushi restaurants   141
Sutton, Robert I.   131–2
swear boxes   238

T-Mobile   183, 186–7
Taylor, David   8, 70
teams
  designing the process
    75–7, 245
  involvement   75–6
  leadership types   238–9
  naïve members   234
  poor casting   238–40,
    254
  R&D   103–4, 226, 247–8
  small teams   212–14
Technical Core concepts
    125–6
technological insights
    103–4
teenage market   14–17, 20,
    103
testing ideas   231–3, 254
Tetrapak   99–100
theatre rules   64, 142–9, 251

location ambience
    145–6
props usage   146–7
prototyping ideas   145
rehearsals   148–9
story-telling   147–8
Streets ice cream   144
three bucket principle   64,
    128–33
  bucket sessions   129–31
  grave-robbing   131–3
  Project Blues   214
Tidd, Joe   30
time factors   36, 80, 244–5
trends
  brainstorming   119, 123,
    250
  insight   100–1, 248

Unilever
  Bertolli   117
  ice cream   13–21, 98, 144
  Peperami   173–5
  Project Blues   209–10,
    212–18
useless products   223–6,
    254

vision
  avoiding pitfalls   231
  clear vision   62–3, 69,
    77–8
  painting   87–91
  see also 'destination'
    envisioning
Vodafone   117–18, 145
VW Beetles   162–3

Walkman, Sony   34–5
wastage of ideas   42–3
water coolers   84

Wella   176
winning mixes   19–20, 157,
    171, 253
    see also 'expander'
        development stage

Woodroffe, Simon   140–2
word games   119–20
Wynett, Craig   163–4

'Yes, and...' comments   119,
    121–2, 238, 250

'Yes, but...' comments
    237–8, 254
Yo!   140–2
Yoplait   183, 198–9

Zara fashions   208

Compiled by Indexing Specialists (UK) Ltd

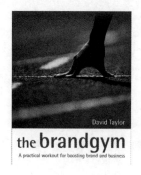

the brandgym: A pratical workout for boosting brand and business

the brandgym is a refreshingly simple, practical guide to brand management and how it can boost business performance. The book reveals the fundamental differences between the winners and losers in the branding battle, illustrated with inside stories from Unilever, Gillette, Apple and others. A programme of eight 'workouts'; will help you raise your own game in key areas such as insight, portfolio strategy, positioning and innovation.

"There is a lot to be learned from Taylor's in-depth examinations, but he is concise and the book is readable. It is written for the practising manager and is short, snappy and practical. This is vigorous, intelligent stuff, from someone who knows what he's talking about." *Marketing Business*

"Taylor's style is refreshingly down-to-earth, with loads of advice on how to grow your brand. The book challenges you to raise your game in key areas such as portfolio strategy and extension. It is a bit like a Hanes car manual for brands. So, if you want to get under the bonnet and do some real work on your brand, not just admire the bodywork, then it's definitely for you." *Marketing*

"More like a mentor than a textbook. Refreshingly straightforward, and easy to apply immediately to day-to-day work, as I am now doing with my team." *Carol Welch, Innovation and Business Director, Cadbury Schweppes*

"A practical, up to date manual on the do's and don'ts of creating powerful brands. Full of great examples, many based on personal experience, and very easy to read. Highly recommended to all brand builders. *Anthony Simon, President Marketing, Unilever Bestfoods*

ISBN: 978-0-470-84710-7 John Wiley & Sons, Ltd.

David Taylor

brandstretch

Why 1 in 2 extensions fail, and how to beat the odds

Brand Stretch: Why 1 in 2 extensions fail and how to beat the odds

Brand extension is a red-hot issue for brand teams and boardrooms alike. Done well, it has the potential to create explosive growth, but the overcrowded extension graveyard shows how hard it is to stretch successfully. This book provides practical help on both the method and mindset needed to boost your chances of winning, illustrated with cases on Dove, Bacardi, Virgin, Starbucks, EasyGroup and many others.

"If this review were to be only two words, they would be "Buy this!". David Taylor's new book is an essential, authoritative and easy-to-understand read for anyone working on a brand or companies exploring the potential for stretching theirs. The theory is supplemented with some outstanding examples" *Media Week*

"David Taylor writes lucidly and is very entertaining. This is important stuff from a leading thinker who sees the pitfalls of the modern fad for brand extension – highly recommended." *The Marketer*

"This is an admirable book, packed with real-life messiness and dozens of examples. Even better, this is a book with a point of view. Taylor is opposed to what he calls the ego-trips of companies such as Virgin and EasyGroup." *Management Today*

"*Brand Stretch* is a triumph of clear thinking, implementable ideas and innovative concepts." *Mark Ritson, Professor of Marketing, London Business School*

"David Taylor's latest book offers a powerful combination of well-researched case studies and practical tips. In a world where the ability to stretch is a key source of competitive advantage, Taylor's advice is required reading." *Andrew Harrison, Marketing Director, Nestle Rowntree*

ISBN: 978-0-470-86211-7 John Wiley & Sons, Ltd.

brand vision
How to Energize Your Team to Drive Business Growth

Brand Vision: How to energize your team to drive business growth

David Taylor's third book lifts the lid on why so many brand visioning projects end in failure: an overly theoretical and complex approach he calls 'strategy tourism'. By contrast, his straightforward, no-nonsense programme will ensure that you end up with an inspiring vision and a hands-on action plan to drive growth. Designed in a highly practical format, *Brand Vision* shows how to lead your team on a step-by-step 'visioning journey' that builds engagement, energy and alignment. Powerful tips, tools and tricks help you start applying the principles to your business today.

"*Brand Vision* cuts to the chase and provides refreshingly candid insights and practical how-to information. That's why it is required reading for the all MBAs and Executives who come to INSEAD to learn about branding. Read it. It will change the way you do business." *Pierre Chandon, Assistant Professor of Marketing, INSEAD*

"This is one of the first books that tackles the real challenges of 21st Century brand building and offers practical solutions to overcome them. If you are looking for help to really understand your customers, position your brand and engage your organisation, you should start with *Brand Vision*." *Mark Ritson, Associate Professor of Marketing, Melbourne Business School*

"If you want to build a truly unique and authentic brand, David's book is a great place to start. It shows how companies like the Geek Squad have created a differentiated point-of-view and inspiring vision, and offers valuable insights on how to create your own." *Robert Stephens, Founder and Chief Inspector, The Geek Squad*

"Keeping a copy of *Brand Vision* close by is like having a legal performance-enhancing drug for your business." *Hugh Burkitt, Chief Executive, The Marketing Society*

ISBN: 978-0-470-02835-3 John Wiley & Sons, Ltd.